Glengarry Schooldays

(Ralph Connor)

Contents

CHAPTER I

THE SPELLING-MATCH

The "Twentieth" school was built of logs hewn on two sides. The cracks were chinked and filled with plaster, which had a curious habit of falling out during the summer months, no one knew how; but somehow the holes always appeared on the boys' side, and being there, were found to be most useful, for as looking out of the window was forbidden, through these holes the boys could catch glimpses of the outer world--glimpses worth catching, too, for all around stood the great forest, the playground of boys and girls during noon-hour and recesses; an enchanted land, peopled, not by fairies, elves, and other shadowy beings of fancy, but with living things, squirrels, and chipmunks, and weasels, chattering ground- hogs, thumping rabbits, and stealthy foxes, not to speak of a host of flying things, from the little gray-bird that twittered its happy nonsense all day, to the big-eyed owl that hooted solemnly when the moon came out. A wonderful place this forest, for children to live in, to know, and to love, and in after days to long for.

It was Friday afternoon, and the long, hot July day was drawing to a weary close. Mischief was in the air, and the master, Archibald Munro, or "Archie Murro," as the boys called him, was holding himself in with a very firm hand, the lines about his mouth showing that he was fighting back the pain which had never quite left him from the day he had twisted his knee out of joint five years ago, in a wrestling match, and which, in his weary moments, gnawed into his vitals. He hated to lose his grip of himself, for then he knew he should have to grow stern and terrifying, and rule these young imps in the forms in front of him by what he called afterwards, in his moments of self-loathing, "sheer brute force," and that he always counted a defeat.

Munro was a born commander. His pale, intellectual face, with its square chin and firm mouth, its noble forehead and deep-set gray eyes, carried a look of such strength and indomitable courage that no boy, however big, ever thought of anything but obedience when the word of command came. He was the only master who had ever been able to control, without at least one appeal to the trustees, the stormy tempers of the young giants that used to come to school in the winter months.

The school never forgot the day when big Bob Fraser "answered back" in class. For, before the words were well out of his lips, the master, with a single stride, was in front of him, and laying two swift, stinging cuts from the rawhide over big Bob's back, commanded, "Hold out your hand!" in a voice so terrible, and with eyes of such blazing light, that before Bob was aware, he shot out his hand

and stood waiting the blow. The school never, in all its history, received such a thrill as the next few moments brought; for while Bob stood waiting, the master's words fell clear-cut upon the dead silence, "No, Robert, you are too big to thrash. You are a man. No man should strike you--and I apologize." And then big Bob forgot his wonted sheepishness and spoke out with a man's voice, "I am sorry I spoke back, sir." And then all the girls began to cry and wipe their eyes with their aprons, while the master and Bob shook hands silently. From that day and hour Bob Fraser would have slain any one offering to make trouble for the master, and Archibald Munro's rule was firmly established.

He was just and impartial in all his decisions, and absolute in his control; and besides, he had the rare faculty of awakening in his pupils an enthusiasm for work inside the school and for sports outside.

But now he was holding himself in, and with set teeth keeping back the pain. The week had been long and hot and trying, and this day had been the worst of all. Through the little dirty panes of the uncurtained windows the hot sun had poured itself in a flood of quivering light all the long day. Only an hour remained of the day, but that hour was to the master the hardest of all the week. The big boys were droning lazily over their books, the little boys, in the forms just below his desk, were bubbling over with spirits-- spirits of whose origin there was no reasonable ground for doubt.

Suddenly Hughie Murray, the minister's boy, a very special imp, held up his hand.

"Well, Hughie," said the master, for the tenth time within the hour replying to the signal.

"Spelling-match!"

The master hesitated. It would be a vast relief, but it was a little like shirking. On all sides, however, hands went up in support of Hughie's proposal, and having hesitated, he felt he must surrender or become terrifying at once.

"Very well," he said; "Margaret Aird and Thomas Finch will act as captains." At once there was a gleeful hubbub. Slates and books were slung into desks.

"Order! or no spelling-match." The alternative was awful enough to quiet even the impish Hughie, who knew the tone carried no idle threat, and who loved a spelling-match with all the ardor of his little fighting soul.

The captains took their places on each side of the school, and with careful deliberation, began the selecting of their men, scanning anxiously the rows of faces looking at the maps or out of the windows and bravely trying to seem unconcerned. Chivalry demanded that Margaret should have first choice. "Hughie Murray!" called out Margaret; for Hughie, though only eight years old, had preternatural gifts in spelling; his mother's training had done that for him. At four he knew every Bible story by heart, and would tolerate no liberties with the text; at six he could read the third reader; at eight he was the best reader in the fifth; and to do him justice, he thought no better of himself for that. It was no trick to read. If he could only run, and climb, and swim, and dive, like the big boys, then he would indeed feel uplifted; but mere spelling and reading, "Huh! that was nothing."

"Ranald Macdonald!" called Thomas Finch, and a big, lanky boy of fifteen or sixteen rose and marched to his place. He was a boy one would look at twice. He was far from handsome. His face was long, and thin, and dark, with a straight nose, and large mouth, and high cheek-bones; but he had fine black eyes, though they were fierce, and had a look in them that suggested the woods and the wild things that live there. But Ranald, though his attendance was spasmodic, and dependent upon the suitability or otherwise of the weather for hunting, was the best speller in the school.

For that reason Margaret would have chosen him, and for another which she would not for worlds have confessed, even to herself. And do you think she would have called Ranald Macdonald to come and stand up beside her before all these boys? Not for the glory of winning the match and carrying the medal for a week. But how gladly would she have given up glory and medal for the joy of it, if she had dared.

At length the choosing was over, and the school ranged in two opposing lines, with Margaret and Thomas at the head of their respective forces, and little Jessie MacRae and Johnnie Aird, with a single big curl on the top of his head, at the foot. It was a point of honor that no blood should be drawn at the first round. To Thomas, who had second choice, fell the right of giving the first word. So to little Jessie, at the foot, he gave "Ox."

"O-x, ox," whispered Jessie, shyly dodging behind her neighbor.

"In!" said Margaret to Johnnie Aird.

"I-s, in," said Johnnie, stoutly.

"Right!" said the master, silencing the shout of laughter. "Next word."

With like gentle courtesies the battle began; but in the second round the little A, B, C's were ruthlessly swept off the field with second-book words, and retired to their seats in supreme exultation, amid the applause of their fellows still left in the fight. After that there was no mercy. It was a give-and-take battle, the successful speller having the right to give the word to the opposite side. The master was umpire, and after his "Next!" had fallen there was no appeal. But if a mistake were made, it was the opponent's part and privilege to correct with all speed, lest a second attempt should succeed.

Steadily, and amid growing excitement, the lines grew less, till there were left on one side, Thomas, with Ranald supporting him, and on the other Margaret, with Hughie beside her, his face pale, and his dark eyes blazing with the light of battle.

Without varying fortune the fight went on. Margaret, still serene, and with only a touch of color in her face, gave out her words with even voice, and spelled her opponent's with calm deliberation. Opposite her Thomas stood, stolid, slow, and wary. He had no nerves to speak of, and the only chance of catching him lay in lulling him off to sleep.

They were now among the deadly words.

"Parallelopiped!" challenged Hughie to Ranald, who met it easily, giving Margaret "hyphen" in return.

"H-y-p-h-e-n," spelled Margaret, and then, with cunning carelessness, gave Thomas "heifer." ("Hypher," she called it.)

Thomas took it lightly.

"H-e-i-p-h-e-r."

Like lightning Hughie was upon him. "H-e-i-f-e-r."

"F-e-r," shouted Thomas. The two yells came almost together.

There was a deep silence. All eyes were turned upon the master.

"I think Hughie was first," he said, slowly. A great sigh swept over the school, and then a wave of applause.

The master held up his hand.

"But it was so very nearly a tie, that if Hughie is willing--"

"All right, sir," cried Hughie, eager for more fight.

But Thomas, in sullen rage, strode to his seat muttering, "I was just as soon anyway." Every one heard and waited, looking at the master.

"The match is over," said the master, quietly. Great disappointment showed in every face.

"There is just one thing better than winning, and that is, taking defeat like a man." His voice was grave, and with just a touch of sadness. The children, sensitive to moods, as is the characteristic of children, felt the touch and sat subdued and silent.

There was no improving of the occasion, but with the same sad gravity the school was dismissed; and the children learned that day one of life's golden lessons--that the man who remains master of himself never knows defeat.

The master stood at the door watching the children go down the slope to the road, and then take their ways north and south, till the forest hid them from his sight.

"Well," he muttered, stretching up his arms and drawing a great breath, "it's over for another week. A pretty near thing, though."

CHAPTER II

THE DEEPOLE

Archibald Munro had a steady purpose in life--to play the man, and to allow no pain of his--and pain never left him long--to spoil his work, or to bring a shadow to the life of any other. And though he had his hard times, no one who could not read the lines about his mouth ever knew how hard they were.

It was this struggle for self-mastery that made him the man he was, and taught him the secrets of nobleness that he taught his pupils with their three "R's"; and this was the best of his work for the Twentieth school.

North and south in front of the school the road ran through the deep forest of great pines, with underbrush of balsam and spruce and silver-birch; but from this main road ran little blazed paths that led to the farm clearings where lay the children's homes. Here and there, set in their massive frames of dark green forest, lay the little farms, the tiny fenced fields surrounding the little log houses and barns. These were the homes of a people simple of heart and manners, but sturdy, clean living, and clear thinking, with their brittle Highland courage toughened to endurance by their long fight with the forest, and with a self-respect born of victory over nature's grimmest of terrors.

A mile straight south of the school stood the manse, which was Hughie's home; two miles straight west Ranald lived; and Thomas Finch two miles north; while the other lads ought to have taken some of the little paths that branched east from the main road. But this evening, with one accord, the boys chose a path that led from the school-house clearing straight southwest through the forest.

What a path that was! Beaten smooth with the passing of many bare feet, it wound through the brush and round the big pines, past the haunts of squirrels, black, gray, and red, past fox holes and woodchuck holes, under birds' nests and bee-trees, and best of all, it brought up at last at the Deep Hole, or "Deepole," as the boys called it.

There were many reasons why the boys should have gone straight home. They were expected home. There were cows to get up from the pasture and to milk, potatoes that needed hoeing, gardens to weed, not to speak of messages and the like. But these were also excellent reasons why the boys should unanimously choose the cool, smooth-beaten, sweet-scented, shady path that wound and twisted through the trees and brush, but led straight to the Deepole. Besides, this was Friday night, it was hot, and they were tired out; the mere thought of the long walk home was intolerable. The Deepole was only two miles away, and "There was lots of time" for anything else. So, with wild whoops, they turned into the shady path and sped through the forest, the big boys in front, with Ranald easily leading, for there was no runner so swift and tireless in all the country-side, and Hughie, with the small boys, panting behind.

On they went, a long, straggling, yelling line, down into the cedar swamp, splashing through the "Little Crick" and up again over the beech ridge, where, in the open woods, the path grew indistinct and was easy to lose; then again among the great pines, where the underbrush was so thick that you could not tell what might be just before, till they pulled up at the old Lumber Camp. The boys always paused at the ruins of the old Lumber Camp. A ruin is ever a place of mystery, but to the old Lumber Camp attached an awful dread, for behind it, in the thickest part of the underbrush, stood the cabin of Alan Gorrach.

Alan's was a name of terror among all the small children of the section. Mothers hushed their crying with, "Alan Gorrach will get you." Alan was a small man, short in the legs, but with long, swinging, sinewy arms. He had a gypsy face, and tangled, long, black hair; and as he walked through the forest he might be heard talking to himself, with wild gesticulations. He was an itinerant cooper by trade, and made for the farmers' wives their butter-tubs and butter-ladles, mincing-bowls and coggies, and for the men, whip-stalks, axe handles, and the like. But in the boys' eyes he was guilty of a horrible iniquity. He was a dog-killer. His chief business was the doing away with dogs of ill-repute in the country; vicious dogs, sheep-killing dogs, egg-sucking dogs, were committed to Alan's dread custody, and often he would be seen leading off his wretched victims to his den in the woods, whence they never returned. It was a current report that he ate them, too. No wonder the boys regarded him with horror mingled with fearful awe.

In broad day, upon the high road, the small boys would boldly fling taunts and stones at Alan, till he would pull out his long, sharp cooper's knife and make at them. But if they met him in the woods they would walk past in trembling and respectful silence, or slip off into hiding in the bush, till he was out of sight.

It was always part of the programme in the exploring of the Lumber Camp for the big boys to steal down the path to Alan's cabin, and peer fearfully through the brush, and then come rushing back to the little boys waiting in the clearing, and crying in terror-stricken stage whispers, "He's coming! He's coming!" set off again through the bush like hunted deer, followed by the panting train of youngsters, with their small hearts thumping hard against their ribs.

In a few minutes the pine woods, with its old Lumber Camp and Alan's fearsome cabin, were left behind; and then down along the flats where the big elms were, and the tall ash-trees, and the alders, the flying, panting line sped on in a final dash, for they could smell the river. In a moment more they were at the Deepole.

O! that Deepole! Where the big creek took a great sweep around before it tore over the rapids and down into the gorge. It was always in cool shade; the great fan-topped elm-trees hung far out over it, and the alders and the willows edged its banks. How cool and clear the dark brown waters looked! And how beautiful the golden mottling on their smooth, flowing surface, where the sun rained down through the over-spreading elm boughs! And the grassy sward where the boys tore off their garments, and whence they raced and plunged, was so green and firm and smooth under foot! And the music of the rapids down in the gorge, and the gurgle of the water where it sucked in under the jam of dead wood before it plunged into the boiling pool farther down! Not that the boys made note of all these delights accessory to the joys of the Deepole itself, but all these helped to weave the spell that the swimming-hole cast over them. Without the spreading elms, without the mottled, golden light upon the cool, deep waters, and without the distant roar of the little rapid, and the soft gurgle at the jam, the Deepole would still have been a place of purest delight, but I doubt if, without these, it would have stolen in among their day dreams in after years, on hot, dusty, weary days, with power to waken in them a vague pain and longing for the sweet, cool woods and the clear, brown waters. Oh, for one plunge! To feel the hug of the waters, their soothing caress, their healing touch! These boys are men now, such as are on the hither side of the darker river, but not a man of them can think, on a hot summer day, of that cool, shaded, mottled Deepole, without a longing in his heart and a lump in his throat.

The last quarter of a mile was always a dead race, for it was a point of distinction to be the first to plunge, and the last few seconds of the race were spent in the preliminaries of the disrobing. A single brace slipped off the shoulder, a flutter of a shirt over the head, a kick of the trousers, and whoop! plunge! "Hurrah! first in." The little boys always waited to admire the first series of plunges, for there were many series before the hour was over, and then they would off to their own crossing, going through a similar performance on a small scale.

What an hour it was! What contests of swimming and diving! What water fights and mud fights! What careering of figures, stark naked, through the rushes and trees! What larks and pranks!

And then the little boys would dress. A simple process, but more difficult by far than the other, for the trousers would stick to the wet feet--no boy would dream of a towel, nor dare to be guilty of such a piece of "stuck-upness"--and the shirt would get wrong side out, or would bundle round the neck, or would cling to the wet shoulders till they had to get on their knees almost to squirm into it. But that over, all was over. The brace, or if the buttons were still there, the braces were easily jerked up on the shoulders, and there you were. Coats, boots, and stockings were superfluous, collars and ties utterly despised.

Then the little ones would gather on the grassy bank to watch the big ones get out, which was a process worth watching.

"Well, I'm going out, boys," one would say.

"Oh, pshaw! let's have another plunge."

"All right. But it's the last, though."

Then a long stream of naked figures would scramble up the bank and rush for the last place. "First out, last in," was the rule, for the boys would much rather jump on some one else than be jumped on themselves. After the long line of naked figures had vanished into the boiling water, one would be seen quietly stealing out and up the bank kicking his feet clean as he stepped off the projecting root onto the grass, when, plunk! a mud ball caught him, and back he must come. It took them full two hours to escape clean from the water, and woe betide the boy last out. On all sides stood boys, little and big, with mud balls ready to fling, till, out of sheer pity, he would be allowed to come forth clean. Then, when all were dressed, and blue and shivering--for two amphibious hours, even on a July day, make one blue--more games would begin, leap-frog, or tag, or jumping, or climbing trees, till they were warm enough to set out for home.

It was as the little ones were playing tag that Hughie came to grief. He was easily king of his company and led the game. Quick as a weasel, swift and wary, he was always the last to be caught. Around the trees, and out and in among the big boys, he led the chase, much to Tom Finch's disgust, who had not forgotten the spelling-match incident. Not that he cared for the defeat, but he still felt the bite in the master's final words, and he carried a grudge against the boy who had been the occasion of his humiliation.

"Keep off!" he cried, angrily, as Hughie swung himself round him. But Hughie paid no heed to Tom's growl, unless, indeed, to repeat his offense, with the result that, as he flew off, Tom caught him a kick that hastened his flight and laid him flat on his back amid the laughter of the boys.

"Tom," said Hughie, gravely and slowly, so that they all stood listening, "do you know what you kick like?"

The boys stood waiting.

"A h-e-i-p-h-e-r."

In a moment Tom had him by the neck, and after a cuff or two, sent him flying, with a warning to keep to himself.

But Hughie, with a saucy answer, was off again on his game, circling as near Tom Finch as he dared, and being as exasperating as possible, till Tom looked as if he would like a chance to pay him off. The chance came, for Hughie, leading the "tag," came flying past Tom and toward the water. Hardly realizing what he was doing, Tom stuck out his foot and caught him flying past, and before any one knew how it had happened, poor Hughie shot far out into the Deepole, lighting fair on his stomach. There was a great shout of laughter, but in a moment every one was calling, "Swim, Hughie!" "Keep your hands down!" "Don't splash like that, you fool!" "Paddle underneath!" But Hughie was far too excited or too stunned by his fall to do anything but splash and sputter, and sink, and rise again, only to sink once more. In a few moments the affair became serious.

The small boys began to cry, and some of the bigger ones to undress, when there was a cry from the elm-tree overhanging the water.

"Run out that board, Don. Quick!"

It was Ranald, who had been swinging up in the highest branches, and had seen what had happened, and was coming down from limb to limb like a squirrel. As he spoke, he dropped from the lowest limb into the water close to where Hughie was splashing wildly.

In an instant, as he rose to the surface, Hughie's arms went round his neck and pulled his head under water. But he was up again, and tugging at Hughie's hands, he cried:

"Don't, Hughie! let go! I'll pull you out. Let go!" But Hughie, half-insensible with terror and with the water he had gulped in, clung with a death-grip.

"Hughie!" gasped Ranald, "you'll drown us both. Oh, Hughie man, let me pull you out, can't you?"

Something in the tone caught Hughie's ear, and he loosed his hold, and Ranald, taking him under the chin, looked round for the board.

By this time Don Cameron was in the water and working the board slowly toward the gasping boys. But now a new danger threatened. The current had gradually carried them toward the log jam, under which the water sucked to the falls below. Once under the jam, no power on earth could save.

"Hurry up, Don!" called out Ranald, anxiously. Then, feeling Hughie beginning to clutch again, he added, cheerily, "It's all right. You'll get us." But his face was gray and his eyes were staring, for over his shoulder he could see the jam and he could feel the suck of the water on his legs.

"Oh, Ranald, you can't do it," sobbed Hughie. "Will I paddle underneath?"

"Yes, yes, paddle hard, Hughie," said Ranald, for the jam was just at his back.

But as he spoke, there was a cry, "Ranald, catch it!" Over the slippery logs of the jam came Tom Finch pushing out a plank.

"Catch it!" he cried, "I'll hold this end solid." And Ranald caught and held fast, and the boys on the bank gave a mighty shout. Soon Don came up with his board, and Tom, catching the end, hauled it up on the rolling logs.

"Hold steady there now!" cried Tom, lying at full length upon the logs; "we'll get you in a minute."

By this time the other boys had pulled a number of boards and planks out of the jam, and laying them across the logs, made a kind of raft upon which the exhausted swimmers were gradually hauled, and then brought safe to shore.

"Oh, Ranald," said Tom, almost weeping, "I didn't mean to--I never thought-- I'm awfully sorry."

"Oh, pshaw!" said Ranald, who was taking off Hughie's shirt preparatory to wringing it, "I know. Besides, it was you who pulled us out. You were doing your best, Don, of course, but we would have gone under the jam but for Tom."

For ten minutes the boys stood going over again the various incidents in the recent dramatic scene, extolling the virtues of Ranald, Don, and Thomas in turn, and imitating, with screams of laughter, Hughie's gulps and splashings while he was fighting for his life. It was their way of expressing their emotions of gratitude and joy, for Hughie was dearly loved by all, though no one would have dared to manifest such weakness.

As they were separating, Hughie whispered to Ranald, "Come home with me, Ranald. I want you." And Ranald, looking down into the little white face, went. It would be many a day before he would get rid of the picture of the white face, with the staring black eyes, floating on the dark brown water beside him, and that was why he went.

When they reached the path to the manse clearing Ranald and Hughie were alone. For some minutes Hughie followed Ranald in silence on a dog-trot, through the brule, dodging round stumps and roots and climbing over fallen trees, till they came to the pasture-field.

"Hold on, Ranald," panted Hughie, putting on a spurt and coming up even with his leader.

"Are you warm enough?" asked Ranald, looking down at the little flushed face.

"You bet!"

"Are you dry?"

"Huh, huh."

"Indeed, you are not too dry," said Ranald, feeling his wet shirt and trousers, "and your mother will be wondering."

"I'll tell her," said Hughie, in a tone of exulting anticipation.

"What!" Ranald stood dead still.

"I'll tell her," replied Hughie. "She'll be awful glad. And she'll be awful thankful to you, Ranald."

Ranald looked at him in amazement.

"I think I will jist be going back now," he said, at length. But Hughie seized him.

"Oh, Ranald, you must come with me."

He had pictured himself telling his mother of Ranald's exploit, and covering his hero with glory. But this was the very thing that Ranald dreaded and hated, and was bound to prevent.

"You will not be going to the Deepole again, I warrant you," Ranald said, with emphasis.

"Not go to the Deepole?"

"No, indeed. Your mother will put an end to that sort of thing."

"Mother! Why not?"

"She will not be wanting to have you drowned."

Hughie laughed scornfully. "You don't know my mother. She's not afraid of--of anything."

"But she will be telling your father."

This was a matter serious enough to give Hughie pause. His father might very likely forbid the Deepole.

"There is no need for telling," suggested Ranald. "And I will just go in for a minute."

"Will you stay for supper?"

Ranald shook his head. The manse kitchen was a bright place, and to see the minister's wife and to hear her talk was to Ranald pure delight. But then, Hughie might tell, and that would be too awful to bear.

"Do, Ranald," pleaded Hughie. "I'll not tell."

"I am not so sure."

"Sure as death!"

Still Ranald hesitated. Hughie grew desperate.

"God may kill me on the spot!" he cried, using the most binding of all oaths known to the boys. This was satisfactory, and Ranald went.

But Hughie was not skilled in deceiving, and especially in deceiving his mother. They were great friends, and Hughie shared all his secrets with her and knew that they were safe, unless they ought to be told. And so, when he caught sight of his mother waiting for him before the door, he left Ranald, and thrilling with the memory of the awful peril through which he had passed, rushed at her, and crying, "Oh, mother!" he flung himself into her arms. "I am so glad to see you again!"

"Why, Hughie, my boy, what's the matter?" said his mother, holding her arms tight about him. "And you are all wet! What is it?" But Hughie held her fast, struggling with himself.

"What is it?" she asked again, turning to Ranald.

"We were running pretty fast--and it is a hot day--and--" But the clear gray-brown eyes were upon him, and Ranald found it difficult to go on.

"Oh, mother, you mustn't ask," cried Hughie; "I promised not to tell."

"Not to tell me, Hughie?" The surprise in the voice was quite too much for Hughie.

"Oh, mother, we did not want to frighten you--and--I promised."

"Then you must keep your promise. Come away in, my boy. Come in, Ranald."

It was her boy's first secret from her. Ranald saw the look of pain in the sweet face, and could not endure it.

"It was just nothing, Mrs. Murray," he began.

"Did you promise, too, Ranald?"

"No, that I did not. And there is nothing much to tell, only Hughie fell into the Deepole and the boys pulled him out!"

"Oh, mother!" exclaimed Hughie, "it was Ranald. He jumped right down from the tree right into the water, and kept me up. You told yourself, Ranald," he continued, delighted to be relieved of his promise; and on he went to give his mother, in his most picturesque style, a description of the whole scene, while Ranald stood looking miserable and ashamed.

"And Ranald was ashamed for me to tell you, and besides, he said you wouldn't let me go to the Deepole again. But you will, won't you mother? And you won't tell father, will you?"

The mother stood listening, with face growing whiter and whiter, till he was done. Then she stooped down over the eager face for some moments, whispering, "My darling, my darling," and then coming to Ranald she held her hand on his shoulder for a moment, while she said, in a voice bravely struggling to be calm, "God reward you, Ranald. God grant my boy may always have so good and brave a friend when he needs."

And from that day Ranald's life was different, for he had bound to him by a tie that nothing could ever break, a friend whose influence followed him, and steadied and lifted him up to greatness, long after the grave had hidden her from men's sight.

CHAPTER III

THE EXAMINATION

The two years of Archibald Munro's regime were the golden age of the school, and for a whole generation "The Section" regarded that period as the standard for comparison in the following years. Munro had a genius for making his pupils work. They threw themselves with enthusiasm into all they undertook-- studies, debate nights, games, and in everything the master was the source of inspiration.

And now his last examination day had come, and the whole Section was stirred with enthusiasm for their master, and with grief at his departure.

The day before examination was spent in "cleaning the school." This semi-annual event, which always preceded the examination, was almost as enjoyable as the examination day itself, if indeed it was not more so. The school met in the morning for a final polish for the morrow's recitations. Then after a speech by the master the little ones were dismissed and allowed to go home though they never by any chance took advantage of this permission. Then the master and the bigger boys and girls set to work to prepare the school for the great day. The boys were told off in sections, some to get dry cedar boughs from the swamp for the big fire outside, over which the iron sugar-kettle was swung to heat the scrubbing water; others off into the woods for balsam-trees for the evergreen decorations; others to draw water and wait upon the scrubbers.

It was a day of delightful excitement, but this year there was below the excitement a deep, warm feeling of love and sadness, as both teacher and pupils thought of to-morrow. There was an additional thrill to the excitement, that the master was to be presented with a gold watch and chain, and that this had been kept a dead secret from him.

What a day it was! With wild whoops the boys went off for the dry cedar and the evergreens, while the girls, looking very housewifely with skirts tucked back and sleeves rolled up, began to sweep and otherwise prepare the room for scrubbing.

The gathering of the evergreens was a delightful labor. High up in the balsam-trees the more daring boys would climb, and then, holding by the swaying top, would swing themselves far out from the trunk and come crashing through the limbs into the deep, soft snow, bringing half the tree with them. What larks they had! What chasing of rabbits along their beaten runways! What fierce and happy snow fights! And then, the triumph of their return, laden with their evergreen trophies, to find the big fire blazing under the great iron kettle and the water boiling, and the girls well on with the scrubbing.

Then, while the girls scrubbed first the benches and desks, and last of all, the floors, the boys washed the windows and put up the evergreen decorations. Every corner had its pillar of green, every window had its frame of green, the old blackboard, the occasion of many a heartache to the unmathematical, was wreathed into loveliness; the maps, with their bewildering boundaries, rivers and mountains, capes, bays and islands, became for once worlds of beauty under the magic touch of the greenery. On the wall just over his desk, the master wrought out in evergreen an arching "WELCOME," but later on, the big girls, with some shy blushing, boldly tacked up underneath an answering "FAREWELL." By the time the short afternoon had faded into the early evening, the school stood, to the eyes of all familiar with the common sordidness of its everyday dress, a picture of artistic loveliness. And after the master's little speech of thanks for their good work that afternoon, and for all their goodness to him, the boys and girls went their ways with that strangely unnameable heart-emptiness that brings an ache to the throat, but somehow makes happier for the ache.

The examination day was the great school event of the year. It was the social function of the Section as well. Toward this event all the school life moved, and its approach was attended by a deepening excitement, shared by children and parents alike, which made a kind of holiday feeling in the air.

The school opened an hour later than ordinarily, and the children came all in their Sunday clothes, the boys feeling stiff and uncomfortable, and regarding each other with looks half shy and half contemptuous, realizing that they were unnatural in each other's sight; the girls with hair in marvelous frizzes and shiny ringlets, with new ribbons, and white aprons over their home-made winsey dresses, carried their unwonted grandeur with an ease and delight that made the boys secretly envy but apparently despise them. The one unpardonable crime with all the boys in that country was that of being "proud." The boy convicted of "shoween off," was utterly contemned by his fellows. Hence, any delight in new clothes or in a finer appearance than usual was carefully avoided.

Ranald always hated new clothes. He felt them an intolerable burden. He did not mind his new homespun, home-made flannel check shirt of mixed red and white, but the heavy fulled-cloth suit made by his Aunt Kirsty felt like a suit of mail. He moved heavily in it and felt queer, and knew that he looked as he felt. The result was that he was in no genial mood, and was on the alert for any indication of levity at his expense.

Hughie, on the contrary, like the girls, delighted in new clothes. His new black suit, made down from one of his father's, with infinite planning and pains by his mother, and finished only at twelve o'clock the night before, gave him unmixed pleasure. And handsome he looked in it. All the little girls proclaimed that in their shy, admiring glances, while the big girls teased and petted and threatened to kiss him. Of course the boys all scorned him and his finery, and tried to "take him down," but Hughie was so unfeignedly pleased with himself, and moved so easily and naturally in his grand attire, and was so cheery and frank and happy, that no one thought of calling him "proud."

Soon after ten the sleighloads began to arrive. It was a mild winter day, when the snow packed well, and there fluttered down through the still air a few lazy flakes, large, soft, and feathery, like bits of the clouds floating white against the blue sky. The sleighs were driven up to the door with a great flourish and jingle of bells, and while the master welcomed the ladies, the fathers and big brothers drove the horses to the shelter of the thick-standing pines, and unhitching them, tied them to the sleigh-boxes, where, blanketed and fed, they remained for the day.

Within an hour the little school-house was packed, the children crowded tight into the long desks, and the visitors on the benches along the walls and in the seats of the big boys and girls. On the platform were such of the trustees as could muster up the necessary courage--old Peter MacRae, who had been a dominie in the Old Country, the young minister and his wife, and the schoolteacher from the "Sixteenth."

First came the wee tots, who, in wide-eyed, serious innocence, went through their letters and their "ox" and "cat" combinations and permutations with great gusto and distinction. Then they were dismissed to their seats by a series of mental arithmetic questions, sums of varying difficulty being propounded, until little white-haired, blue-eyed Johnnie Aird, with the single big curl on the top of his head, was left alone.

"One and one, Johnnie?" said the master, smiling down at the rosy face.

"Three," promptly replied Johnnie, and retired to his seat amid the delighted applause of visitors and pupils, and followed by the proud, fond, albeit almost tearful, gaze of his mother. He was her baby, born long after her other babies had grown up into sturdy youth, and all the dearer for that.

Then up through the Readers, till the Fifth was reached, the examination progressed, each class being handed over to the charge of a visitor, who forthwith went upon examination as truly as did the class.

"Fifth class!" In due order the class marched up to the chalk line on the floor in front of the master's desk, and stood waiting.

The reading lesson was Fitz-Greene Halleck's "Marco Bozzaris," a selection of considerable dramatic power, and calling for a somewhat spirited rendering. The master would not have chosen this lesson, but he had laid down the rule that there was to be no special drilling of the pupils for an exhibition, but that the school should be seen doing its every-day work; and in the reading, the lessons for the previous day were to be those of the examination day. By an evil fortune, the reading for the day was the dramatic "Marco Bozzaris." The master shivered inwardly as he thought of the possibility of Thomas Finch, with his stolidly monotonous voice, being called upon to read the thrilling lines recording the panic-stricken death-cry of the Turk: "To arms! They come! The Greek! The Greek!" But Thomas, by careful plodding, had climbed to fourth place, and the danger lay in the third verse.

"Will you take this class, Mr. MacRae?" said the master, handing him the book. He knew that the dominie was not interested in the art of reading beyond the point of correct pronunciation, and hence he hoped the class might get off easily. The dominie took the book reluctantly. What he desired was the "arith-MET-ic" class, and did not care to be "put off" with mere reading.

"Well, Ranald, let us hear you," he rather growled. Ranald went at his work with quiet confidence; he knew all the words.

"Page 187, Marco Bozzaris.

"At midnight in his guarded tent, The Turk lay dreaming of the hour When Greece, her knee in suppliance bent, Should tremble at his power."

And so on steadily to the end of his verse.

"Next!"

The next was "Betsy Dan," the daughter of Dan Campbell, of "The Island." Now, Betsy Dan was very red in hair and face, very shy and very nervous, and always on the point of giggles. It was a trial to her to read on ordinary days, but to-day it was almost more than she could bear. To make matters worse, sitting immediately behind her, and sheltered from the eye of the master, sat Jimmie Cameron, Don's youngest brother. Jimmie was always on the alert for mischief, and ever ready to go off into fits of laughter, which he managed to check only by grabbing tight hold of his nose. Just now he was busy pulling at the strings of Betsy Dan's apron with one hand, while with the other he was hanging onto his nose, and swaying in paroxysms of laughter.

Very red in the face, Betsy Dan began her verse.

"At midnight in the forest shades, Bozzaris--"

Pause, while Betsy Dan clutched behind her.

"--Bozzaris ranged--"

("Tchik! tchik!") a snicker from Jimmie in the rear.

"--his Suliote band, True as the steel of--"

("im-im,") Betsy Dan struggles with her giggles.

"Elizabeth!" The master's voice is stern and sharp.

Betsy Dan bridles up, while Jimmie is momentarily sobered by the master's tone.

"True as the steel of their tried blades, Heroes in heart and hand. There had the Persians thousands stood--"

("Tchik! tchik! tchik,") a long snicker from Jimmie, whose nose cannot be kept quite in control. It is becoming too much for poor Betsy Dan, whose lips begin to twitch.

"There--"

("im-im, thit-tit-tit,") Betsy Dan is making mighty efforts to hold in her giggles.

"--had the glad earth (tchik!) drunk their blood, On old Pl-a-a-t-t-e-a-'s day."

Whack! whack!

"Elizabeth Campbell!" The master's tone was quite terrible.

"I don't care! He won't leave me alone. He's just--just (sob) pu--pulling at me (sob) all the time."

By this time Betsy's apron was up to her eyes, and her sobs were quite tempestuous.

"James, stand up!" Jimmie slowly rose, red with laughter, and covered with confusion.

"I-I-I di-dn't touch her!" he protested.

"O--h!" said little Aleck Sinclair, who had been enjoying Jimmie's prank hugely; "he was--"

"That'll do, Aleck, I didn't ask you. James is quite able to tell me himself. Now, James!"

"I-I-I was only just doing that," said Jimmie, sober enough now, and terrified at the results of his mischief.

"Doing what?" said the master, repressing a smile at Jimmie's woebegone face.

"Just-just that!" and Jimmie touched gingerly with the point of his finger the bows of Betsy Dan's apron-strings.

"Oh, I see. You were annoying Elizabeth while she was reading. No wonder she found it difficult. Now, do you think that was very nice?"

Jimmie twisted himself into a semicircle.

"N-o-o."

"Come here, James!" Jimmie looked frightened, came round the class, and up to the master.

"Now, then," continued the master, facing Jimmie round in front of Betsy Dan, who was still using her apron upon her eyes, "tell Elizabeth you are sorry."

Jimmie stood in an agony of silent awkwardness, curving himself in varying directions.

"Are you sorry?"

"Y-e-e-s."

"Well, tell her so."

Jimmie drew a long breath and braced himself for the ordeal. He stood a moment or two, working his eyes up shyly from Betsy Dan's shoes to her face, caught her glancing at him from behind her apron, and began, "I-I-I'm (tchik! tchik) sor-ry," (tchik). Betsy Dan's look was too much for the little chap's gravity.

A roar swept over the school-house. Even the grim dominie's face relaxed.

"Go to your seat and behave yourself," said the master, giving Jimmie a slight cuff. "Now, Margaret, let us go on."

Margaret's was the difficult verse. But to Margaret's quiet voice and gentle heart, anything like shriek or battle-cry was foreign enough, so with even tone, and unmodulated by any shade of passion, she read the cry, "To arms! They come! The Greek! The Greek!" Nor was her voice to be moved from its gentle, monotonous flow even by the battle-cry of Bozzaris, "Strike! till the last armed foe expires!"

"Next," said the dominie, glad to get on with his task.

The master breathed freely, when, alas for his hopes, the minister spoke up.

"But, Margaret, do you think Bozzaris cheered his men in so gentle a voice as that?"

Margaret smiled sweetly, but remained silent, glad to get over the verse.

"Wouldn't you like to try it again?" suggested the minister.

Margaret flushed up at once.

"Oh, no," said his wife, who had noticed Margaret's flushing face. "Girls are not supposed to be soldiers, are they, Margaret?"

Margaret flashed a grateful look at her.

"That's a boy's verse."

"Ay! that it is," said the old dominie; "and I would wish very much that Mrs. Murray would conduct this class."

But the minister's wife would not hear of it, protesting that the dominie could do it much better. The old man, however, insisted, saying that he had no great liking for this part of the examination, and would wish to reserve himself, with the master's permission, for the "arith-MET-ic" class.

Mrs. Murray, seeing that it would please the dominie, took the book, with a spot of color coming in her delicate, high-bred face.

"You must all do your best now, to help me," she said, with a smile that brought an answering smile flashing along the line. Even Thomas Finch allowed his stolid face a gleam of intelligent sympathy, which, however, he immediately suppressed, for he remembered that the next turn was his, and that he must be getting himself into the appearance of dogged desperation which he considered suitable to a reading exercise.

"Now, Thomas," said the minister's wife, sweetly, and Thomas plunged heavily.

"They fought like brave men, long--"

"Oh, Thomas, I think we will try that man's verse again, with the cries of battle in it, you know. I am sure you can do that well."

It was all the same to Thomas. There were no words he could not spell, and he saw no reason why he should not do that verse as well as any other. So, with an extra knitting of his eyebrows, he set forth doggedly.

"An-hour-passed-on-the-Turk-awoke-that-bright-dream-was-his-last."

Thomas's voice fell with the unvarying regularity of the beat of a trip-hammer.

"He-woke-to-hear-his-sentries-shriek-to-arms-they-come-the-Greek-   the-Greek-he-woke--"

"But, Thomas, wait a minute. You see you must speak these words, 'To arms! They come!' differently from the others. These words were shrieked by the sentries, and you must show that in your reading."

"Speak them out, man," said the minister, sharply, and a little nervously, fearing that his wife had undertaken too great a task, and hating to see her defeated.

"Now, Thomas," said Mrs. Murray, "try again. And remember the sentries shrieked these words, 'To arms!' and so on."

Thomas squared his shoulders, spread his feet apart, added a wrinkle to his frown, and a deeper note of desperation to his tone, and began again.

"An-hour-passed-on-the-Turk-awoke-that-bright-dream-was--"

The master shuddered.

"Now, Thomas, excuse me. That's better, but we can improve that yet." Mrs. Murray was not to be beaten. The attention of the whole school, even to Jimmie Cameron, as well as that of the visitors, was now concentrated upon the event.

"See," she went on, "each phrase by itself. 'An hour passed on: the Turk awoke.' Now, try that far."

Again Thomas tried, this time with complete success. The visitors applauded.

"Ah, that's it, Thomas. I was sure you could do it."

Thomas relaxed a little, but not unduly. He was not sure what was yet before him.

"Now we will get that 'sentries shriek.' See, Thomas, like this a little," and she read the words with fine expression.

"You must put more pith, more force, into those words, Thomas. Speak out, man!" interjected the minister, who was wishing it was all over.

"Now, Thomas, I think this will be the last time. You have done very well, but I feel sure you can do better."

The minister's wife looked at Thomas as she said this, with so fascinating a smile that the frown on Thomas' face deepened into a hideous scowl, and he planted himself with a do-or-die expression in every angle of his solid frame. Realizing the extreme necessity of the moment, he pitched his voice several tones higher than ever before in his life inside a house and before people, and made his final attempt.

"An-hour-passed-on: the-Turk-awoke: That-bright-dream-WAS-his-last."

And now, feeling that the crisis was upon him, and confusing speed with intensity, and sound with passion, he rushed his words, with ever-increasing speed, into a wild yell.

"He-woke-to-hear-his-sentries-shriek-to-arms-they come-the-Greek- THE-GREEK!"

There was a moment of startled stillness, then, "tchik! tchik!" It was Jimmie again, holding his nose and swaying in a vain effort to control a paroxysm of snickers at Thomas' unusual outburst.

It was like a match to powder. Again the whole school burst into a roar of uncontrollable laughter. Even the minister, the master, and the dominie, could not resist. The only faces unmoved were those of Thomas Finch and the minister's wife. He had tried his best, and it was to please her, and she knew it.

A swift, shamed glance round, and his eyes rested on her face. That face was sweet and grave as she leaned toward him, and said, "Thank you, Thomas. That was well done." And Thomas, still looking at her, flushed to his hair roots and down the back of his neck, while the scowl on his forehead faded into a frown, and then into smoothness.

"And if you always try your best like that, Thomas, you will be a great and good man some day."

Her voice was low and soft, as if intended for him alone, but in the sudden silence that followed the laughter it thrilled to every heart in the room, and Thomas was surprised to find himself trying to swallow a lump in his throat, and to keep his eyes from blinking; and in his face, stolid and heavy, a new expression was struggling for utterance. "Here, take me," it said; "all that I have is thine," and later days brought the opportunity to prove it.

The rest of the reading lesson passed without incident. Indeed, there pervaded the whole school that feeling of reaction which always succeeds an emotional climax. The master decided to omit the geography and grammar classes, which should have immediately followed, and have dinner at once, and so allow both children and visitors time to recover tone for the spelling and arithmetic of the afternoon.

The dinner was an elaborate and appalling variety of pies and cakes, served by the big girls and their sisters, who had recently left school, and who consequently bore themselves with all proper dignity and importance. Two of the boys passed round a pail of water and a tin cup, that all the thirsty might drink. From hand to hand, and from lip to lip the cup passed, with a fine contempt of microbes. The only point of etiquette insisted upon was that no "leavings" should be allowed to remain in the cup or thrown back into the pail, but should be carefully flung upon the floor.

There had been examination feasts in pre-historic days in the Twentieth school, when the boys indulged in free fights at long range, using as missiles remnants of pie crust and cake, whose consistency rendered them deadly enough to "bloody" a nose or black an eye. But these barbaric encounters ceased with Archie Munro's advent, and now the boys vied with each other in "minding their manners." Not only was there no snatching of food or exhibition of greediness, but there was a severe repression of any apparent eagerness for the tempting dainties, lest it should be suspected that such were unusual at home. Even the little boys felt that it would be bad manners to take a second piece of cake or pie unless specially pressed; but their eager, bulging eyes revealed only too plainly their heart's desire, and the kindly waiters knew their duty sufficiently to urge a second, third, and fourth supply of the toothsome currant or berry pie, the solid fruit cake, or the oily doughnut, till the point was reached where desire failed.

"Have some more, Jimmie. Have a doughnut," said the master, who had been admiring Jimmie's gastronomic achievements.

"He's had ten a'ready," shouted little Aleck Sinclair, Jimmie's special confidant.

Jimmie smiled in conscious pride, but remained silent.

"What! eaten ten doughnuts?" asked the master, feigning alarm.

"He's got four in his pocket, too," said Aleck, in triumph.

"He's got a pie in his own pocket," retorted Jimmie, driven to retaliate.

"A pie!" exclaimed the master. "Better take it out. A pocket's not the best place for a pie. Why don't you eat it, Aleck?"

"I can't," lamented Aleck. "I'm full up."

"He said he's nearly busted," said Jimmie, anxiously. "He's got a pain here," pointing to his left eye. The bigger boys and some of the visitors who had gathered round shouted with laughter.

"Oh, pshaw, Aleck!" said the master, encouragingly, "that's all right. As long as the pain is as high up as your eye you'll recover. I tell you what, put your pie down on the desk here, Jimmie will take care of it, and run down to the gate and tell Don I want him."

Aleck, with great care and considerable difficulty, extracted from his pocket a segment of black currant pie, hopelessly battered, but still intact. He regarded it fondly for a moment or two, and then, with a very dubious look at Jimmie, ran away on his errand for the master.

It took him some little time to find Don, and meanwhile the master's attention was drawn away by his duty to the visitors. The pie left to Jimmie's care had an unfortunately tempting fringe of loose pieces about it that marred its symmetry. Jimmie proceeded to trim it into shape. So absorbed did he become in this trimming process, that before he realized what he was about, he woke suddenly to the startling fact that the pie had shrunk into a comparatively insignificant size. It would be worse than useless to save the mutilated remains for Aleck; there was nothing for it now but to get the reproachful remnant out of the way. He was so busily occupied with this praiseworthy proceeding that he failed to notice Aleck enter the room, flushed with his race, eager and once more empty.

Arriving at his seat, he came upon Jimmie engaged in devouring the pie left in his charge. With a cry of dismay and rage he flung himself upon the little gourmand, and after a short struggle, secured the precious pie; but alas, bereft of its most delicious part--it was picked clean of its currants. For a moment he gazed, grief-stricken, at the leathery, viscous remnant in his hand. Then, with a wrathful exclamation, "Here, then, you can just take it then, you big pig, you!" He seized Jimmie by the neck, and jammed the sticky pie crust on his face, where it stuck like an adhesive plaster. Jimmie, taken by surprise, and rendered nerveless by the pangs of an accusing conscience, made no resistance, but set up a howl that attracted the attention of the master and the whole company.

"Why, Jimmie!" exclaimed the master, removing the doughy mixture from the little lad's face, "what on earth are you trying to do? What is wrong, Aleck?"

"He ate my pie," said Aleck, defiantly.

"Ate it? Well, apparently not. But never mind, Aleck, we shall get you another pie."

"There isn't any more," said Aleck, mournfully; "that was the last piece."

"Oh, well, we shall find something else just as good," said the master, going off after one of the big girls; and returning with a doughnut and a peculiarly deadly looking piece of fruit cake, he succeeded in comforting the disappointed and still indignant Aleck.

The afternoon was given to the more serious part of the school work--writing, arithmetic, and spelling, while, for those whose ambitions extended beyond the limits of the public school, the master had begun a Euclid class, which was at once his despair and his pride. In the Twentieth school of that date there was no waste of the children's time in foolish and fantastic branches of study, in showy exercises and accomplishments, whose display was at once ruinous to the nerves of the visitors, and to the self-respect and modesty of the children. The ideal of the school was to fit the children for the struggle into which their lives would thrust them, so that the boy who could spell and read and cipher was supposed to be ready for his life work. Those whose ambition led them into the subtleties of Euclid's problems and theorems were supposed to be in preparation for somewhat higher spheres of life.

Through the various classes of arithmetic the examination proceeded, the little ones struggling with great seriousness through their addition and subtraction sums, and being wrought up to the highest pitch of excitement by their contest for the first place. By the time the fifth class was reached, the air was heavy with the feeling of battle. Indeed, it was amazing to note how the master had succeeded in arousing in the whole school an intense spirit of emulation. From little Johnnie Aird up to Thomas Finch, the pupils carried the hearts of soldiers.

Through fractions, the "Rule of Three," percentages, and stocks, the senior class swept with a trail of glory. In vain old Peter MacRae strewed their path with his favorite posers. The brilliant achievements of the class seemed to sink him deeper and deeper into the gloom of discontent, while the master, the minister and his wife, as well as the visitors, could not conceal their delight. As a last resort the old dominie sought to stem their victorious career with his famous problem in Practice, and to his huge enjoyment, one after another of the class had to acknowledge defeat. The truth was, the master had passed lightly over this rule in the arithmetic, considering the solution of problems by the method of Practice as a little antiquated, and hardly worthy of much study. The failure of the class, however, brought the dominie his hour of triumph, and so complete had been the success of the examination that the master was abundantly willing that he should enjoy it.

Then followed the judging of the copy-books. The best and cleanest book in each class was given the proud distinction of a testimonial written upon the first blank page, with the date of the examination and the signatures of the examiners attached. It was afterwards borne home in triumph by the happy owner, to be stored among the family archives, and perhaps among the sacred things that mothers keep in their holy of holies.

After the copy-books had been duly appraised, there followed an hour in which the excitement of the day reached its highest mark. The whole school, with such of the visitors as could be persuaded to join, were ranged in opposing ranks in the deadly conflict of a spelling-match. The master, the teacher from the Sixteenth, and even the minister's wife, yielded to the tremendous pressure of public demand that they should enter the fray. The contest had a most dramatic finish, and it was felt that the extreme possibility of enthusiasm and excitement was reached when the minister's wife spelled down the teacher from the Sixteenth, who every one knew, was the champion speller of all the country that lay toward the Front, and had a special private armory of deadly missiles laid up against just such a conflict as this. The tumultuous triumph of the children was not to be controlled. Again and again they followed Hughie in wild yells, not only because his mother was a great favorite with them all, but because she had wrested a victory from the champion of the Front, for the Front, in all matters pertaining to culture and fashion, thought itself quite superior to the more backwoods country of the Twentieth.

It was with no small difficulty that the master brought the school to such a degree of order that the closing speeches could be received with becoming respect and attention. The trustees, according to custom, were invited to express their opinion upon the examination, and upon school matters generally. The chairman, John Cameron, "Long John," as he was called, broke the ice after much persuasion, and slowly rising from the desk into which he had compressed his long, lank form, he made his speech. Long John was a great admirer of the master, but for all that, and perhaps because of that, he allowed himself no warmer words of commendation than that he was well pleased with the way in which the children had conducted themselves. "They have done credit to themselves," he said, "and to their teacher. And indeed I am sorry he is leaving us, for, so far, I have heard no complaints in the Section."

The other trustees followed in the path thus blazed out for them by Long John. They were all well pleased with the examination, and they were all sorry to lose the master, and they had heard no complaints. It was perfectly understood that no words of praise could add to the high testimony that they "had heard no complaints."

The dominie's speech was a little more elaborate. Somewhat reluctantly he acknowledged that the school had acquitted itself with "very considerable credit," especially the "arith-MET-ic" class, and indeed, considering all the circumstances, Mr. Munro was to be congratulated upon the results of his work in the Section. But the minister's warm expression of delight at the day's proceedings, and of regret at the departure of the master, more than atoned for the trustees' cautious testimony, and the dominie's somewhat grudging praise.

Then came the moment of the day. A great stillness fell upon the school as the master rose to make his farewell speech. But before he could say a word, up from their seats walked Betsy Dan and Thomas Finch, and ranged themselves before him. The whole assemblage tingled with suppressed excitement. The great secret with which they had been burdening themselves for the past few weeks was now to be out. Slowly Thomas extracted the manuscript from his trousers pocket, and smoothed out its many folds, while Betsy Dan waited nervously in the rear.

"Oh, why did they set Thomas to this?" whispered the minister's wife, who had a profound sense of humor. The truth was, the choice of the school had fallen upon Ranald and Margaret Aird. Margaret was quite willing to act, but Ranald refused point-blank, and privately persuaded Thomas to accept the honor in his stead. To this Thomas agreed, all the more readily that Margaret, whom he adored from a respectful distance, was to be his partner. But Margaret, who would gladly have been associated with Ranald, on the suggestion that Thomas should take his place, put up her lower lip in that symbol of scorn so effective with girls, but which no boy has ever yet accomplished, and declared that indeed, and she would see that Tom Finch far enough, which plainly meant "no." Consequently they had to fall back upon Betsy Dan, who, in addition to being excessively nervous, was extremely good-natured. And Thomas, though he would greatly have preferred Margaret as his assistant, was quite ready to accept Betsy Dan.

The interval of waiting while Thomas deliberately smoothed out the creases of the paper was exceedingly hard upon Betsy Dan, whose face grew redder each moment. Jimmie Cameron, too, who realized that the occasion was one of unusual solemnity, was gazing at Thomas with intense interest growing into amusement, and was holding his fingers in readiness to seize his nose, and so check any explosion of snickers. Just as Thomas had got the last fold of his paper straightened out, and was turning it right end up, it somehow slipped through his fingers to the floor. This was too much for Jimmie, who only saved himself from utter disgrace by promptly seizing his nose and holding on for dear life. Thomas gave Jimmie a passing glare and straightened himself up for his work. With a furious frown he cleared his throat and began in a solemn, deep-toned roar, "Dear teacher, learning with regret that you are about to sever your connection," etc., etc. All went well until he came to the words, "We beg you to accept this gift, not for its intrinsic value," etc., which was the cue for Betsy Dan. But Betsy Dan was engaged in terrorizing Jimmie, and failed to come in, till, after an awful pause, Thomas gave her a sharp nudge, and whispered audibly, "Give it to him, you gowk." Poor Betsy Dan, in sudden confusion, whipped her hand out from under her apron, and thrusting a box at the master, said hurriedly, "Here it is, sir." As Thomas solemnly concluded his address, a smile ran round the room, while Jimmie doubled himself up in his efforts to suppress a tempest of snickers.

The master, however, seemed to see nothing humorous in the situation, but bowing gravely to Thomas and Betsy Dan, he said, kindly, "Thank you, Thomas! Thank you, Elizabeth!" Something in his tone brought the school to attention, and even Jimmie forgot to have regard to his nose. For a few moments the master stood looking upon the faces of his pupils, dwelling upon them one by one, till his eyes rested upon the wee tots in the front seat, looking at him with eyes of innocent and serious wonder. Then he thanked the children for their gift in a few simple words, assuring them that he should always wear the watch with pride and grateful remembrance of the Twentieth school, and of his happy days among them.

But when he came to say his words of farewell, and to thank them for their goodness to him, and their loyal backing of him while he was their teacher, his voice grew husky, and for a moment wavered. Then, after a pause, he spoke of what had been his ideal among them. "It is a good thing to have your minds trained and stored with useful knowledge, but there are better things than that. To learn honor, truth, and right; to be manly and womanly; to be self-controlled and brave and gentle--these are better than all possible stores of learning; and if I have taught you these at all, then I have done what I most wished to do. I have often failed, and I have often been discouraged, and might have given up were it not for the help I received at my worst times from our minister and from Mrs. Murray, who often saved me from despair."

A sudden flush tinged the grave, beautiful face of the minister's young wife. A light filled her eyes as the master said these words, for she remembered days when the young man's pain was almost greater than he could bear, and when he was near to giving up.

When the master ceased, the minister spoke a few words in appreciation of the work he had done in the school, and in the whole Section, during his three years' stay among them, and expressed his conviction that many a young lad would grow into a better man because he had known Archibald Munro, and some of them would never forget what he had done for them.

By this time all the big girls and many of the visitors were openly weeping. The boys were looking straight in front of them, their faces set in an appearance of savage gloom, for they knew well how near they were to "acting like the girls."

After a short prayer by the minister, the children filed out past the master, who stood at the door and shook hands with them one by one. When the big boys, and the young men who had gone to school in the winter months, came to say good by, they shook hands silently, and then stood close about him as if hating to let him go. He had caught for them in many a close base-ball match; he had saved their goal in many a fierce shinny fight with the Front; and while he had ruled them with an iron rule, he had always treated them fairly. He had never failed them; he had never weakened; he had always been a man among them. No wonder they stood close about him and hated to lose him. Suddenly big Bob Fraser called out in a husky voice, "Three cheers for the captain!" and every one was glad of the chance to let himself out in a roar. And that was the last of the farewells.

CHAPTER IV

THE NEW MASTER

Right in front of the school door, and some little distance from it, in the midst of a clump of maples, stood an old beech-tree with a dead top, and half-way down where a limb had once been and had rotted off, a hole. Inside this hole two very respectable but thoroughly impudent red squirrels had made their nest. The hole led into the dead heart of the tree, which had been hollowed out with pains so as to make a roomy, cosy home, which the squirrels had lined with fur and moss, and which was well stored with beechnuts from the tree, their winter's provisions.

Between the boys and the squirrels there existed an armed neutrality. It was understood among the boys that nothing worse than snowballs was to be used in their war with the squirrels, while with the squirrels it was a matter of honor that they should put reasonable limits to their profanity. But there were times when the relations became strained, and hence the holidays were no less welcome to the squirrels than to the boys.

To the squirrels this had been a day of unusual anxiety, for the school had taken up again after its two weeks' holidays, and the boys were a little more inquisitive than usual, and unfortunately, the snow happened to be good for packing. It had been a bad day for nerves, and Mr. Bushy, as the boys called him, found it impossible to keep his tail in one position for more than one second at a time. It was in vain that his more sedate and self- controlled partner in life remonstrated with him and urged a more philosophic mind.

"It's all very well for you, my dear," Mr. Bushy was saying, rather crossly I am afraid, "to urge a philosophic mind, but if you had the responsibility of the family upon you--Goodness gracious! Owls and weasels! What in all the woods is that?"

"Can't be the wolves," said Mrs. Bushy, placidly, "it's too early for them."

"Might have known," replied her husband, quite crossly; "of course it's those boys. I wonder why they let them out of school at all. Why can't they keep them in where it is warm? It always seems to me a very silly thing anyway, for them to keep rushing out of their hole in that stupid fashion. What they do in there I am sure I don't know. It isn't the least like a nest. I've seen inside of it. There isn't a thing to eat, nor a bit of hair or moss. They just go in and out again."

"Well, my dear," said his wife, soothingly, "you can hardly expect them to know as much as people with a wider outlook. We must remember they are only ground people."

"That's just it!" grumbled Mr. Bushy. "I only wish they would just keep to themselves and on the ground where they belong, but they have the impudence to come lumbering up here into our tree."

"Oh, well," replied his partner, calmly, "you must acknowledge they do not disturb our nest."

"And a good thing for them, too," chattered Mr. Bushy, fiercely, smoothing out his whiskers and showing his sharp front teeth, at which Mrs. Bushy smiled gently behind her tail.

"But what are they doing now?" she inquired.

"Oh, they are going off into the woods," said Mr. Bushy, who had issued from his hole and was sitting up on a convenient crotch. "And I declare!" he said, in amazed tones, "they haven't thrown one snowball at me. Something must be badly wrong with them. Wonder what it is? This is quite unprecedented."

At this Mrs. Bushy ventured carefully out to observe the extraordinary phenomenon, for the boys were actually making their way to the gate, the smaller ones with much noisy shouting, but the big boys soberly enough engaged in earnest conversation. It was their first day of the new master, and such a day as quite "flabbergastrated," as Don Cameron said, even the oldest of them. But of course Mr. and Mrs. Bushy knew nothing of this, and could only marvel.

"Murdie," cried Hughie to Don's big brother, who with Bob Fraser, Ranald Macdonald, and Thomas Finch was walking slowly toward the gate, "you won't forget to ask your pa for an excuse if you happen to be late to-morrow, will you?"

Murdie paid no attention.

"You won't forget your excuse, Murdie," continued Hughie, poking him in the back.

Murdie suddenly turned, caught him by the neck and the seat of his trousers, and threw him head first into a drift, from which he emerged wrathful and sputtering.

"Well, I hope you do," continued Hughie, "and then you'll catch it. And mind you," he went on, circling round to get in front of him, "if you want to ask big Bob there for his knife, mind you hold up your hand first." Murdie only grinned at him.

The new master had begun the day by enunciating the regulations under which the school was to be administered. They made rather a formidable list, but two of them seemed to the boys to have gone beyond the limits of all that was outrageous and absurd. There was to be no speaking during school hours, and if a boy should desire to ask a question of his neighbor, he was to hold up his hand and get permission from the master. But worse than all, and more absurd than all, was the regulation that all late comers and absentees were to bring written excuses from parents or guardians.

"Guardian," Thomas Finch had grunted, "what's that?"

"Your grandmother," whispered Don back.

It was not Don's reply that brought Thomas into disgrace this first day of the new master's rule, it was the vision of big Murdie Cameron walking up to the desk with an excuse for lateness, which he had obtained from Long John, his father. This vision breaking suddenly in upon the solemnity of Thomas Finch's mind, had sent him into a snort of laughter, not more to the surprise of the school than of himself. The gravity of the school had not been greatly helped by Thomas sheepish answer to the master's indignant question, "What did you do that for, sir?"

"I didn't; it did itself."

On the whole, the opening day had not been a success. As a matter of fact, it was almost too much to expect that it should be anything but a failure. There was a kind of settled if unspoken opinion among the children that no master could ever fill Archibald Munro's place in the school. Indeed, it was felt to be a kind of impertinence for any man to attempt such a thing. And further, there was a secret sentiment among the boys that loyalty to the old master's memory demanded an attitude of unsympathetic opposition to the one who came to take his place. It did not help the situation that the new master was unaware of this state of mind. He was buoyed up by the sentiments of enthusiastic admiration and approval that he carried with him in the testimonials from his last board of trustees in town, with which sentiments he fully agreed, and hence he greeted the pupils of the little backwoods school with an airy condescension that reduced the school to a condition of speechless and indignant astonishment. The school was prepared to tolerate the man who should presume to succeed their former master, if sufficiently humble, but certainly not to accept airy condescension from him.

"Does he think we're babies?" asked Don, indignantly.

"And did you see him trying to chop at recess?" (REE'cis, Hughie called it.) "He couldn't hit twice in the same place."

"And he asked me if that beech there was a maple," said Bob Fraser, in deep disgust.

"Oh, shut up your gab!" said Ranald, suddenly. "Give the man a chance, anyway."

"Will YOU bring an excuse when you're absent, Ranald?" asked Hughie.

"And where would I be getting it?" asked Ranald, grimly, and all the boys realized the absurdity of expecting a written excuse for Ranald's absence from his father. Macdonald Dubh was not a man to be bothered with such trifles.

"You might get it from your Aunt Kirsty, Ranald," said Don, slyly. The boys shouted at the suggestion.

"And she could do it well enough if it would be necessary," said Ranald, facing square round on Don, and throwing up his head after his manner when battle was in the air, while the red blood showed in his dark cheek and his eyes lit up with a fierce gleam. Don read the danger signal.

"I'm not saying she couldn't," he hurried to say, apologetically, "but it would be funny, wouldn't it?"

"Well," said Ranald, relenting and smiling a little, "it would be keeping her busy at times."

"When the deer are running, eh, Ranald," said Murdie, good- naturedly. "But Ranald's right, boys," he continued, "give the man a chance, say I."

"There's our bells," cried Thomas Finch, as the deep, musical boom of the Finch's sleigh-bells came through the bush. "Come on, Hughie, we'll get them at the cross." And followed by Hughie and the boys from the north, he set off for the north cross-roads, where they would meet the Finch's bob-sleighs coming empty from the saw-mill, to the great surprise and unalloyed delight of Mr. and Mrs. Bushy, who from their crotch in the old beech had watched with some anxiety the boys' unusual conduct.

"There they are, Hughie," called Thomas, as the sleighs came out into the open at the crossroads. "They'll wait for us. They know you're coming," he yelled, encouragingly, for the big boys had left the smaller ones, a panting train, far in the rear, and were piling themselves upon the Finch's sleighs, with never a "by your leave" to William John--familiarly known as Billy Jack--Thomas' eldest brother, who drove the Finch's team.

Thomas' home lay a mile north and another east from the Twentieth cross-roads, but the winter road by which they hauled saw-logs to the mill, cut right through the forest, where the deep snow packed hard into a smooth track, covering roots and logs and mud holes, and making a perfect surface for the sleighs, however heavily loaded, except where here and there the pitch-holes or cahots came. These cahots, by the way, though they became, especially toward the spring, a serious annoyance to teamsters, only added another to the delights that a sleigh-ride held for the boys.

To Hughie, the ride this evening was blissful to an unspeakable degree. He was overflowing with new sensations. He was going to spend the night with Thomas, for one thing, and Thomas as his host was quite a new and different person from the Thomas of the school. The minister's wife, ever since the examination day, had taken a deeper interest in Thomas, and determined that something should be made out of the solemn, stolid, slow-moving boy. Partly for this reason she had yielded to Hughie's eager pleading, backing up the invitation brought by Thomas himself and delivered in an agony of red-faced confusion, that Hughie should be allowed to go home with him for the night. Partly, too, because she was glad that Hughie should see something of the Finch's home, and especially of the dark-faced, dark-eyed little woman who so silently and unobtrusively, but so efficiently, administered her home, her family, and their affairs, and especially her husband, without suspicion on his part that anything of the kind was being done.

In addition to the joy that Hughie had in Thomas in his new role as host, this winter road was full of wonder and delight, as were all roads and paths that wound right through the heart of the bush. The regular made-up roads, with the forest cut back beyond the ditches at the sides, were a great weariness to Hughie, except indeed, in the springtime, when these ditches were running full with sun-lit water, over the mottled clay bottom and gravelly ripples. But the bush roads and paths, summer and winter, were filled with things of wonder and of beauty, and this particular winter road of the Finch's was best of all to Hughie, for it was quite new to him, and besides, it led right through the mysterious, big pine swamp and over the butternut ridge, beyond which lay the Finch's farm. Balsam-trees, tamarack, spruce, and cedar made up the thick underbrush of the pine swamp, white birch, white ash, and black were thickly sprinkled through it, but high above these lesser trees towered the white pines, lifting their great, tufted crests in lonely grandeur, seeming like kings among meaner men. Here and there the rabbit runways, packed into hard little paths, crossed the road and disappeared under the thick spruces and balsams; here and there, the sly, single track of the fox, or the deep hoof-mark of the deer, led off into unknown depths on either side. Hughie, sitting up on the bolster of the front bob beside Billy Jack, for even the big boys recognized his right, as Thomas' guest, to that coveted place, listened with eager face and wide- open eyes to Billy Jack's remarks upon the forest and its strange people.

One thing else added to Hughie's keen enjoyment of the ride. Billy Jack's bays were always in the finest of fettle, and pulled hard on the lines, and were rarely allowed the rapture of a gallop. But when the swamp was passed and the road came to the more open butternut ridge, Billy Jack shook the lines over their backs and let them out. Their response was superb to witness, and brought Hughie some moments of ecstatic rapture. Along the hard-packed road that wound about among the big butternuts, the rangey bays sped at a flat gallop, bounding clear over the cahots, the booming of the bells and the rattling of the chains furnishing an exhilarating accompaniment to the swift, swaying motion, while the children clung for dear life to the bob-sleighs and to each other. It was all Billy Jack could do to get his team down to a trot by the time they reached the clearing, for there the going was perilous, and besides, it was just as well that his father should not witness any signs on Billy Jack's part of the folly that he was inclined to attribute to the rising generation. So steadily enough the bays trotted up the lane and between long lines of green cordwood on one side and a hay-stack on the other, into the yard, and swinging round the big straw-stack that faced the open shed, and was flanked on the right by the cow-stable and hog-pen, and on the left by the horse-stable, came to a full stop at their own stable door.

"Thomas, you take Hughie into the house to get warm, till I unhitch," said Billy Jack, with the feeling that courtesy to the minister's son demanded this attention. But Hughie, rejecting this proposition with scorn, pushed Thomas aside and set himself to unhitch the S-hook on the outside trace of the nigh bay. It was one of Hughie's grievances, and a very sore point with him, that his father's people would insist on treating him in the privileged manner they thought proper to his father's son, and his chief ambition was to stand upon his own legs and to fare like other boys. So he scorned Billy Jack's suggestion, and while some of the children scurried about the stacks for a little romp before setting off for their homes, which some of them, for the sake of the ride, had left far behind, Hughie devoted himself to the unhitching of the team with Billy Jack. And so quick was he in his movements, and so fearless of the horses, that he had his side unhitched and was struggling with the breast-strap before Billy Jack had finished with his horse.

"Man! you're a regular farmer," said Billy Jack, admiringly, "only you're too quick for the rest of us."

Hughie, still struggling with the breast-strap, found his heart swell with pride. To be a farmer was his present dream.

"But that's too heavy for you," continued Billy Jack. "Here, let down the tongue first."

"Pshaw!" said Hughie, disgusted at his exhibition of ignorance, "I knew that tongue ought to come out first, but I forgot."

"Oh, well, it's just as good that way, but not quite so easy," said Billy Jack, with doubtful consistency.

It took Hughie but a few minutes after the tongue was let down to unfasten his end of the neck-yoke and the cross-lines, and he was beginning at his hame-strap, always a difficult buckle, when Billy Jack called out, "Hold on there! You're too quick for me. We'll make them carry their own harness into the stable. Don't believe in making a horse of myself." Billy Jack was something of a humorist.

The Finch homestead was a model of finished neatness. Order was its law. Outside, the stables, barns, stacks, the very wood-piles, evidenced that law. Within, the house and its belongings and affairs were perfect in their harmonious arrangement. The whole establishment, without and within, gave token of the unremitting care of one organizing mind, for, from dark to dark, while others might have their moments of rest and careless ease, "the little mother," as Billy Jack called her, was ever on guard, and all the machinery of house and farm moved smoothly and to purpose because of that unsleeping care. She was last to bed and first to stir, and Billy Jack declared that she used to put the cats to sleep at night, and waken up the roosters in the morning. And through it all her face remained serene, and her voice flowed in quiet tones. Billy Jack adored her with all the might of his big heart and body. Thomas, slow of motion as of expression, found in her the center of his somewhat sluggish being. Jessac, the little dark-faced maiden of nine years, whose face was the very replica of her mother's, knew nothing in the world dearer, albeit in her daily little housewifely tasks she felt the gentle pressure of that steadfast mind and unyielding purpose. Her husband regarded her with a curious mingling of reverence and defiance, for Donald Finch was an obstinate man, with a man's love of authority, and a Scotchman's sense of his right to rule in his own house. But while he talked much about his authority, and made a great show of absolutism with his family, he was secretly conscious that another will than his had really kept things moving about the farm; for he had long ago learned that his wife was always right, while he might often be wrong, and that, withal her soft words and gentle ways, hers was a will like steel.

Besides the law of order, another law ruled in the Finch household-- the law of work. The days were filled with work, for they each had their share to do, and bore the sole responsibility for its being well done. If the cows failed in their milk, or the fat cattle were not up to the mark, the father felt the reproach as his; to Billy Jack fell the care and handling of the horses; Thomas took charge of the pigs, and the getting of wood and water for the house; little Jessac had her daily task of "sorting the rooms," and when the days were too stormy or the snow too deep for school, she had in addition her stent of knitting or of winding the yarn for the weaver. To the mother fell all the rest. At the cooking and the cleaning, and the making and the mending, all fine arts with her, she diligently toiled from long before dawn till after all the rest were abed. But besides these and other daily household duties there were, in their various seasons, the jam and jelly, the pumpkin and squash preserves, the butter-making and cheese-making, and more than all, the long, long work with the wool. Billy Jack used to say that the little mother followed that wool from the backs of her sheep to the backs of her family, and hated to let the weaver have his turn at it. What with the washing and the oiling of it, the carding and the spinning, the twisting and the winding, she never seemed to be done. And then, when it came back from the weaver in great webs of fulled-cloth and flannel and winsey, there was all the cutting, shaping, and sewing before the family could get it on their backs. True, the tailor was called in to help, but though he declared he worked no place else as he worked at the Finch's, it was Billy Jack's openly expressed opinion that "he worked his jaw more than his needle, for at meal-times he gave his needle a rest."

But though Hughie, of course, knew nothing of this toiling and moiling, he was distinctly conscious of an air of tidiness and comfort and quiet, and was keenly alive to the fact that there was a splendid supper waiting him when he got in from the stables with the others, "hungry as a wild-cat," as Billy jack expressed it. And that WAS a supper! Fried ribs of fresh pork, and hashed potatoes, hot and brown, followed by buckwheat pancakes, hot and brown, with maple syrup. There was tea for the father and mother with their oat cakes, but for the children no such luxury, only the choice of buttermilk or sweet milk. Hughie, it is true, was offered tea, but he promptly declined, for though he loved it well enough, it was sufficient reason for him that Thomas had none. It took, however, all the grace out of his declining, that Mr. Finch remarked in gruff pleasantry, "What would a boy want with tea!" The supper was a very solemn meal. They were all too busy to talk, at least so Hughie felt, and as for himself, he was only afraid lest the others should "push back" before he had satisfied the terrible craving within him.

After supper the books were taken, and in Gaelic, for though Donald Finch was perfectly able in English for business and ordinary affairs of life, when it came to the worship of God, he found that only in the ancient mother tongue could he "get liberty." As Hughie listened to the solemn reading, and then to the prayer that followed, though he could understand only a word now and again, he was greatly impressed with the rhythmic, solemn cadence of the voice, and as he glanced through his fingers at the old man's face, he was surprised to find how completely it had changed. It was no longer the face of the stern and stubborn autocrat, but of an earnest, humble, reverent man of God; and Hughie, looking at him, wondered if he would not be altogether nicer with his wife and boys after that prayer was done. He had yet to learn how obstinate and even hard a man can be and still have a great "gift in prayer."

From the old man's face, Hughie's glance wandered to his wife's, and there was held fascinated. For the first time Hughie thought it was beautiful, and more than that, he was startled to find that it reminded him of his mother's. At once he closed his eyes, for he felt as if he had been prying where he had no right.

After the prayer was over they all drew about the glowing polished kitchen stove with the open front, and set themselves to enjoy that hour which, more than any other, helps to weave into the memory the thoughts and feelings that in after days are associated with home. Old Donald drew forth his pipe, a pleased expectation upon his face, and after cutting enough tobacco from the black plug which he pulled from his trousers pocket, he rolled it fine, with deliberation, and packed it carefully into his briar-root pipe, from which dangled a tin cap; then drawing out some live coals from the fire, he with a quick motion picked one up, set it upon the top of the tobacco, and holding it there with his bare finger until Hughie was sure he would burn himself, puffed with hard, smacking puffs, but with a more comfortable expression than Hughie had yet seen him wear. Then, when it was fairly lit, he knocked off the coal, packed down the tobacco, put on the little tin cap, and sat back in his covered arm-chair, and came as near beaming upon the world as ever he allowed himself to come.

"Here, Jessac," he said to the little dark-faced maiden slipping about the table under the mother's silent direction. Jessac glanced at her mother and hesitated. Then, apparently reading her mother's face, she said, "In a minute, da," and seizing the broom, which was much taller than herself, she began to brush up the crumbs about the table with amazing deftness. This task completed, and the crumbs being thrown into the pig's barrel which stood in the woodshed just outside the door, Jessac set her broom in the corner, hung up the dust-pan on its proper nail behind the stove, and then, running to her father, climbed up on his knee and snuggled down into his arms for an hour's luxurious laziness before the fire. Hughie gazed in amazement at her temerity, for Donald Finch was not a man to take liberties with; but as he gazed, he wondered the more, for again the face of the stern old man was transformed.

"Be quaet now, lassie. Hear me now, I am telling you," he admonished the little girl in his arms, while there flowed over his face a look of half-shamed delight that seemed to fill up and smooth out all its severe lines.

Hughie was still gazing and wondering when the old man, catching his earnest, wide-open gaze, broke forth suddenly, in a voice nearly jovial, "Well, lad, so you have taken up the school again. You will be having a fine time of it altogether."

The lad, startled more by the joviality of his manner than by the suddenness of his speech, hastily replied, "Indeed, we are not, then."

"What! what!" replied the old man, returning to his normal aspect of severity. "Do you not know that you have great privileges now?"

"Huh!" grunted Hughie. "If we had Archie Munro again."

"And what is wrong with the new man?"

"Oh, I don't know. He's not a bit nice. He's--"

"Too many rules," said Thomas, slowly.

"Aha!" said his father, with a note of triumph in his tone; "so that's it, is it? He will be bringing you to the mark, I warrant you. And indeed it's high time, for I doubt Archie Munro was just a little soft with you."

The old man's tone was aggravating enough, but his reference to the old master was too much for Hughie, and even Thomas was moved to words more than was his wont in his father's presence.

"He has too many rules," repeated Thomas, stolidly, "and they will not be kept."

"And he is as proud as he can be," continued Hughie. "Comes along with his cane and his stand-up collar, and lifts his hat off to the big girls, and--and--och! he's just as stuck-up as anything!" Hughie's vocabulary was not equal to his contempt.

"There will not be much wrong with his cane in the Twentieth School, I dare say," went on the old man, grimly. "As for lifting his hat, it is time some of them were learning manners. When I was a boy we were made to mind our manners, I can tell you."

"So are we!" replied Hughie, hotly; "but we don't go shoween off like that! And then himself and his rules!" Hughie's disgust was quite unutterable.

"Rules!" exclaimed the old man. "Ay, that is what is the trouble."

"Well," said Hughie, with a spice of mischief, "if Thomas is late for school he will have to bring a note of excuse."

"Very good indeed. And why should he be late at all?"

"And if any one wants a pencil he can't ask for it unless he gets permission from the master."

"Capital!" said the old man, rubbing his hands delightedly. "He's the right sort, whatever."

"And if you keep Thomas home a day or a week, you will have to write to the master about it," continued Hughie.

"And what for, pray?" said the old man, hastily. "May I not keep-- but-- Yes, that's a very fine rule, too. It will keep the boys from the woods, I am thinking."

"But think of big Murdie Cameron holding up his hand to ask leave to speak to Bob Fraser!"

"And why not indeed? If he's not too big to be in school he's not too big for that. Man alive! you should have seen the master in my school days lay the lads over the forms and warm their backs to them."

"As big as Murdie?"

"Ay, and bigger. And what's more, he would send for them to their homes, and bring them strapped to a wheel-barrow. Yon was a master for you!"

Hughie snorted. "Huh! I tell you what, we wouldn't stand that. And we won't stand this man either."

"And what will you be doing now, Hughie?" quizzed the old man.

"Well," said Hughie, reddening at the sarcasm, "I will not do much, but the big boys will just carry him out."

"And who will be daring to do that, Hughie?"

"Well, Murdie, and Bob Fraser, and Curly Ross, and Don, and--and Thomas, there," added Hughie, fearing to hurt Thomas' feelings by leaving him out.

"Ay," said the old man, shutting his lips tight on his pipestem and puffing with a smacking noise, "let me catch Thomas at that!"

"And I would help, too," said Hughie, valiantly, fearing he had exposed his friend, and wishing to share his danger.

"Well, your father would be seeing to that," said the old man, with great satisfaction, feeling that Hughie's discipline might be safely left in the minister's hands.

There was a pause of a few moments, and then a quiet voice inquired gently, "He will be a very big man, Hughie, I suppose."

"Oh, just ordinary," said Hughie, innocently, turning to Mrs. Finch.

"Oh, then, they will not be requiring you and Thomas, I am thinking, to carry him out." At which Hughie and Billy Jack and Jessac laughed aloud, but Thomas and his father only looked stolidly into the fire.

"Come, Thomas," said his mother, "take your fiddle a bit. Hughie will like a tune." There was no need of any further discussing the new master.

But Thomas was very shy about his fiddle, and besides he was not in a mood for it; his father's words had rasped him. It took the united persuasions of Billy Jack and Jessac and Hughie to get the fiddle into Thomas' hands, but after a few tuning scrapes all shyness and moodiness vanished, and soon the reels and strathspeys were dropping from Thomas' flying fingers in a way that set Hughie's blood tingling. But when the fiddler struck into Money Musk, Billy Jack signed Jessac to him, and whispering to her, set her out on the middle of the floor.

"Aw, I don't like to," said Jessac, twisting her apron into her mouth.

"Come away, Jessac," said her mother, quietly, "do your best." And Jessac, laying aside shyness, went at her Highland reel with the same serious earnestness she gave to her tidying or her knitting. Daintily she tripped the twenty-four steps of that intricate, ancient dance of the Celt people, whirling, balancing, poising, snapping her fingers, and twinkling her feet in the true Highland style, till once more her father's face smoothed out its wrinkles, and beamed like a harvest moon. Hughie gazed, uncertain whether to allow himself to admire Jessac's performance, or to regard it with a boy's scorn, as she was only a girl. And yet he could not escape the fascination of the swift, rhythmic movement of the neat, twinkling feet.

"Well done, Jessac, lass," said her father, proudly. "But what would the minister be saying at such frivolity?" he added, glancing at Hughie.

"Huh! he can do it himself well enough," said Hughie, "and I tell you what, I only wish I could do it."

"I'll show you," said Jessac, shyly, but for the first time in his life Hughie's courage failed, and though he would have given much to be able to make his feet twinkle through the mazes of the Highland reel, he could not bring himself to accept teaching from Jessac. If it had only been Thomas or Billy Jack who had offered, he would soon enough have been on the floor. For a moment he hesitated, then with a sudden inspiration, he cried, "All right. Do it again. I'll watch." But the mother said quietly, "I think that will do, Jessac. And I am afraid your father will be going with cold hands if you don't hurry with those mitts." And Jessac put up her lip with the true girl's grimace and went away for her knitting, to Hughie's disappointment and relief.

Soon Billy Jack took down the tin lantern, pierced with holes into curious patterns, through which the candle-light rayed forth, and went out to bed the horses. In spite of protests from all the family, Hughie set forth with him, carrying the lantern and feeling very much the farmer, while Billy Jack took two pails of boiled oats and barley, with a mixture of flax-seed, which was supposed to give to the Finch's team their famous and superior gloss. When they returned from the stable they found in the kitchen Thomas, who was rubbing a composition of tallow and bees-wax into his boots to make them water-proof, and the mother, who was going about setting the table for the breakfast.

"Too bad you have to go to bed, mother," said Billy Jack, struggling with his boot-jack. "You might just go on getting the breakfast, and what a fine start that would give you for the day."

"You hurry, William John, to bed with that poor lad. What would his mother say? He must be fairly exhausted."

"I'm not a bit tired," said Hughie, brightly, his face radiant with the delight of his new experiences.

"You will need all your sleep, my boy," said the mother, kindly, "for we rise early here. But," she added, "you will lie till the boys are through with their work, and Thomas will waken you for your breakfast."

"Indeed, no! I'm going to get up," announced Hughie.

"But, Hughie," said Billy Jack, seriously, "if you and Thomas are going to carry out that man to-morrow, you will need a mighty lot of sleep to-night."

"Hush, William John," said the mother to her eldest son, "you mustn't tease Hughie. And it's not good to be saying such things, even in fun, to boys like Thomas and Hughie."

"That's true, mother, for they're rather fierce already."

"Indeed, they are not that. And I am sure they will do nothing that will shame their parents."

To this Hughie made no reply. It was no easy matter to harmonize the thought of his parents with the exploit of ejecting the master from the school, so he only said good night, and went off with the silent Thomas to bed. But in the visions of his head which haunted him the night long, racing horses and little girls with tossing curls and twinkling feet were strangely mingled with wild conflicts with the new master; and it seemed to him that he had hardly dropped off to sleep, when he was awake again to see Thomas standing beside him with a candle in his hand, announcing that breakfast was ready.

"Have you been out to the stable?" he eagerly inquired, and Thomas nodded. In great disappointment and a little shamefacedly he made his appearance at the breakfast-table.

It seemed to Hughie as if it must be still the night before, for it was quite dark outside. He had never had breakfast by candle-light before in his life, and he felt as if it all were still a part of his dreams, until he found himself sitting beside Billy Jack on a load of saw-logs, waving good by to the group at the door, the old man, whose face in the gray morning light had resumed its wonted severe look, the quiet, little dark-faced woman, smiling kindly at him and bidding him come again, and the little maid at her side with the dark ringlets, who glanced at him from behind the shelter of her mother's skirts, with shy boldness.

As Hughie was saying his good bys, he was thinking most of the twinkling feet and the tossing curls, and so he added to his farewells, "Good by, Jessac. I'm going to learn that reel from you some day," and then, turning about, he straight-way forgot all about her and her reel, for Billy Jack's horses were pawing to be off, and rolling their solemn bells, while their breath rose in white clouds above their heads, wreathing their manes in hoary rime.

"Git-ep, lads," said Billy Jack, hauling his lines taut and flourishing his whip. The bays straightened their backs, hung for a few moments on their tugs, for the load had frozen fast during the night, and then moved off at a smart trot, the bells solemnly booming out, and the sleighs creaking over the frosty snow.

"Man!" said Hughie, enthusiastically, "I wish I could draw logs all winter."

"It's not too bad a job on a day like this," assented Billy Jack. And indeed, any one might envy him the work on such a morning. Over the treetops the rays of the sun were beginning to shoot their rosy darts up into the sky, and to flood the clearing with light that sparkled and shimmered upon the frost particles, glittering upon and glorifying snow and trees, and even the stumps and fences. Around the clearing stood the forest, dark and still, except for the frost reports that now and then rang out like pistol shots. To Hughie, the early morning invested the forest with a new beauty and a new wonder. The dim light of the dawning day deepened the silence, so that involuntarily he hushed his voice in speaking, and the deep-toned roll of the sleigh-bells seemed to smite upon that dim, solemn quiet with startling blows. On either side the balsams and spruces, with their mantles of snow, stood like white-swathed sentinels on guard--silent, motionless, alert. Hughie looked to see them move as the team drove past.

As they left the more open butternut ridge and descended into the depths of the big pine swamp, the dim light faded into deeper gloom, and Hughie felt as if he were in church, and an awe gathered upon him.

"It's awful still," he said to Billy Jack in a low tone, and Billy Jack, catching the look in the boy's face, checked the light word upon his lips, and gazed around into the deep forest glooms with new eyes. The mystery and wonder of the forest had never struck him before. It had hitherto been to him a place for hunting or for getting big saw-logs. But to-day he saw it with Hughie's eyes, and felt the majesty of its beauty and silence. For a long time they drove without a word.

"Say, it's mighty fine, isn't it?" he said, adopting Hughie's low tone.

"Splendid!" exclaimed Hughie. "My! I could just hug those big trees. They look at me like--like your mother, don't they, or mine?" But this was beyond Billy Jack.

"Like my mother?"

"Yes, you know, quiet and--and--kind, and nice."

"Yes," said Thomas, breaking in for the first time, "that's just it. They do look, sure enough, like my mother and yours. They have both got that look."

"Git-ep!" said Billy Jack to his team. "These fellows'll be ketchin' something bad if we don't get into the open soon. Shouldn't wonder if they've got 'em already, making out their mothers like an old white pine. Git-ep, I say!"

"Oh, pshaw!" said Hughie, "you know what I mean."

"Not much I don't. But it don't matter so long as you're feelin' all right. This swamp's rather bad for the groojums."

"What?" Hughie's eyes began to open wide as he glanced into the forest.

"The groojums. Never heard of them things? They ketch a fellow in places like this when it's gettin' on towards midnight, and about daylight it's almost as bad."

"What are they like?" asked Hughie, upon whom the spell of the forest lay.

"Oh, mighty queer. Always crawl up on your back, and ye can't help twistin' round."

Hughie glanced at Thomas and was at once relieved.

"Oh, pshaw! Billy Jack, you can't fool me. I know you."

"I guess you're safe enough now. They don't bother you much in the clearing," said Billy Jack, encouragingly.

"Oh, fiddle! I'm not afraid."

"Nobody is in the open, and especially in the daytime."

"Oh, I don't care for your old groojums."

"Guess you care more for your new boss yonder, eh?" said Billy Jack, nodding toward the school-house, which now came into view.

"Oh," said Hughie, with a groan, "I just hate going to-day."

"You'll be all right when you get there," said Billy Jack, cheerfully. "It's like goin' in swimmin'."

Soon they were at the cross-roads.

"Good by, Billy Jack," said Hughie, feeling as if he had been on a long, long visit. "I've had an awfully good time, and I'd like to go back with you."

"Wish you would," said Billy Jack, heartily. "Come again soon. And don't carry out the master to-day. It looks like a storm; he might get cold."

"He had better mind out, then," cried Hughie after Billy Jack, and set off with Thomas for the school. But neither Hughie nor Thomas had any idea of the thrilling experiences awaiting them in the Twentieth School before the week was done.

CHAPTER V

THE CRISIS

The first days of that week were days of strife. Murdie Cameron and Bob Fraser and the other big boys succeeded in keeping in line with the master's rules and regulations. They were careful never to be late, and so saved themselves the degradation of bringing an excuse. But the smaller boys set themselves to make the master's life a burden, and succeeded beyond their highest expectations, for the master was quick of temper, and was determined at all costs to exact full and prompt obedience. There was more flogging done those first six days than during any six months of Archie Munro's rule. Sometimes the floggings amounted to little, but sometimes they were serious, and when those fell upon the smaller boys, the girls would weep and the bigger boys would grind their teeth and swear.

The situation became so acute that Murdie Cameron and the big boys decided that they would quit the school. They were afraid the temptation to throw the master out would some day be more than they could bear, and for men who had played their part, not without credit, in the Scotch River fights, to carry out the master would have been an exploit hardly worthy of them. So, in dignified contempt of the master and his rules, they left the school after the third day.

Their absence did not help matters much; indeed, the master appeared to be relieved, and proceeded to tame the school into submission. It was little Jimmie Cameron who precipitated the crisis. Jimmie's nose, upon which he relied when struggling with his snickers, had an unpleasant trick of failing him at critical moments, and of letting out explosive snorts of the most disturbing kind. He had finally been warned that upon his next outburst punishment would fall.

It was Friday afternoon, the drowsy hour just before recess, while the master was explaining to the listless Euclid class the mysteries of the forty-seventh proposition, that suddenly a snort of unusual violence burst upon the school. Immediately every eye was upon the master, for all had heard and had noted his threat to Jimmie.

"James, was that you, sir?"

There was no answer, except such as could be gathered from Jimmie's very red and very shamed face.

"James, stand up!"

Jimmie wriggled to his feet, and stood a heap of various angles.

"Now, James, you remember what I promised you? Come here, sir!"

Jimmie came slowly to the front, growing paler at each step, and stood with a dazed look on his face, before the master. He had never been thrashed in all his life. At home the big brothers might cuff him good-naturedly, or his mother thump him on the head with her thimble, but a serious whipping was to him an unknown horror.

The master drew forth his heavy black strap with impressive deliberation and ominous silence. The preparations for punishment were so elaborate and imposing that the big boys guessed that the punishment itself would not amount to much. Not so Jimmie. He stood numb with fear and horrible expectation. The master lifted up the strap.

"James, hold out your hand!"

Jimmie promptly clutched his hand behind his back.

"Hold out your hand, sir, at once!" No answer.

"James, you must do as you are told. Your punishment for disobedience will be much severer than for laughing." But Jimmie stood pale, silent, with his hands tight clasped behind his back.

The master stepped forward, and grasping the little boy's arm, tried to pull his hand to the front; but Jimmie, with a roar like that of a young bull, threw himself flat on his face on the floor and put his hands under him. The school burst into a laugh of triumph, which increased the master's embarrassment and rage.

"Silence!" he said, "or it will be a worse matter for some of you than for James."

Then turning his attention to Jimmie, be lifted him from the floor and tried to pull out his hand. But Jimmie kept his arms folded tight across his breast, roaring vigorously the while, and saying over and over, "Go away from me! Go away from me, I tell you! I'm not taking anything to do with you."

The big boys were enjoying the thing immensely. The master's rage was deepening in proportion. He felt it would never do to be beaten. His whole authority was at stake.

"Now, James," he reasoned, "you see you are only making it worse for yourself. I cannot allow any disobedience in the school. You must hold out your hand."

But Jimmie, realizing that he had come off best in the first round, stood doggedly sniffing, his arms still folded tight.

"Now, James, I shall give you one more chance. Hold out your hand."

Jimmie remained like a statue.

Whack! came the heavy strap over his shoulders. At once Jimmie set up his refrain, "Go away from me, I tell you! I'm not taking anything to do with you!"

Whack! whack! whack! fell the strap with successive blows, each heavier than the last. There was no longer any laughing in the school. The affair was growing serious. The girls were beginning to sob, and the bigger boys to grow pale.

"Now, James, will you hold out your hand? You see how much worse you are making it for yourself," said the master, who was heartily sick of the struggle, which he felt to be undignified, and the result of which he feared was dubious.

But Jimmie only kept up his cry, now punctuated with sobs, "I'm-- not--taking--anything--to do--with--you."

"Jimmie, listen to me," said the master. "You must hold out your hand. I cannot have boys refusing to obey me in this school." But Jimmie caught the entreaty in the tone, and knowing that the battle was nearly over, kept obstinately silent.

"Well, then," said the master, suddenly, "you must take it," and lifting the strap, he laid it with such sharp emphasis over Jimmie's shoulders that Jimmie's voice rose in a wilder roar than usual, and the girls burst into audible weeping.

Suddenly, above all the hubbub, rose a voice, clear and sharp.

"Stop!" It was Thomas Finch, of all people, standing with face white and tense, and regarding the master with steady eyes.

The school gazed thunderstruck at the usually slow and stolid Thomas.

"What do you mean, sir?" said the master, gladly turning from Jimmie. But

Thomas stood silent, as much surprised as the master at his sudden exclamation.

He stood hesitating for a moment, and then said, "You can thrash me in his place. He's a little chap, and has never been thrashed."

The master misunderstood his hesitation for fear, pushed Jimmie aside, threw down his strap, and seized a birch rod.

"Come forward, sir! I'll put an end to your insubordination, at any rate. Hold out your hand!"

Thomas held out his hand till the master finished one birch rod.

"The other hand, sir!"

Another birch rod was used up, but Thomas neither uttered a sound nor made a move till the master had done, then he asked, in a strained voice, "Were you going to give Jimmie all that, sir?"

The master caught the biting sneer in the tone, and lost himself completely.

"Do you dare to answer me back?" he cried. He opened his desk, took out a rawhide, and without waiting to ask for his hand, began to lay the rawhide about Thomas's shoulders and legs, till he was out of breath.

"Now, perhaps you will learn your place, sir," he said.

"Thank you," said Thomas, looking him steadily in the eye.

"You are welcome. And I'll give you as much more whenever you show that you need it." The slight laugh with which he closed this brutal speech made Thomas wince as he had not during his whole terrible thrashing, but still he had not a word to say.

"Now, James, come here!" said the master, turning to Jimmie. "You see what happens when a boy is insubordinate." Jimmie came trembling. "Hold out your hand!" Out came Jimmie's hand at once. Whack! fell the strap.

"The other!"

"Stop it!" roared Thomas. "I took his thrashing."

"The other!" said the master, ignoring Thomas.

With a curious savage snarl Thomas sprung at him. The master, however, was on the alert, and swinging round, met him with a straight facer between the eyes, and Thomas went to the floor.

"Aha! my boy! I'll teach you something you have yet to learn."

For answer came another cry, "Come on, boys!" It was Ranald Macdonald, coming over the seats, followed by Don Cameron, Billy Ross, and some smaller boys. The master turned to meet them.

"Come along!" he said, backing up to his desk. "But I warn you it's not a strap or a rawhide I shall use."

Ranald paid no attention to his words, but came straight toward him, and when at arm's length, sprung at him with the cry, "Horo, boys!"

But before he could lay his hands upon the master, he received a blow straight on the bridge of the nose that staggered him back, stunned and bleeding. By this time Thomas was up again, and rushing in was received in like manner, and fell back over a bench.

"How do you like it, boys?" smiled the master. "Come right along."

The boys obeyed his invitation, approaching him, but more warily, and awaiting their chance to rush. Suddenly Thomas, with a savage snarl, put his head down and rushed in beneath the master's guard, paid no attention to the heavy blow he received on the head, and locking his arms round the master's middle, buried his head close into his chest.

At once Ranald and Billy Ross threw themselves upon the struggling pair and carried them to the floor, the master underneath. There was a few moments of fierce struggling, and then the master lay still, with the four boys holding him down for dear life.

It was Thomas who assumed command.

"Don't choke him so, Ranald," he said. "And clear out of the way, all you girls and little chaps."

"What are you going to do, Thomas?" asked Don, acknowledging Thomas's new-born leadership.

"Tie him up," said Thomas. "Get me a sash."

At once two or three little boys rushed to the hooks and brought one or two of the knitted sashes that hung there, and Thomas proceeded to tie the master's legs.

While he was thus busily engaged, a shadow darkened the door, and a voice exclaimed, "What is all this about?" It was the minister, who had been driving past and had come upon the terrified, weeping children rushing home.

"Is that you, Thomas? And you, Don?"

The boys let go their hold and stood up, shamed but defiant.

Immediately the master was on his feet, and with a swift, fierce blow, caught Thomas on the chin. Thomas, taken off his guard, fell with a thud on the floor.

"Stop that, young man!" said the minister, catching his arm. "That's a coward's blow."

"Hands off!" said the master, shaking himself free and squaring up to him.

"Ye would, would ye?" said the minister, gripping him by the neck and shaking him as he might a child. "Lift ye're hand to me, would ye? I'll break you're back to ye, and that I will." So saying, the minister seized him by the arms and held him absolutely helpless. The master ceased to struggle, and put down his hands.

"Ay, ye'd better, my man," said the minister, giving him a fling backward.

Meantime Don had been holding snow to Thomas's head, and had brought him round.

"Now, then," said the minister to the boys, "what does all this mean?"

The boys were all silent, but the master spoke.

"It is a case of rank and impudent insubordination, sir, and I demand the expulsion of those impudent rascals."

"Well, sir," said the minister, "be sure there will be a thorough investigation, and I greatly misjudge the case if there are not faults on both sides. And for one thing, the man who can strike such a cowardly blow as you did a moment ago would not be unlikely to be guilty of injustice and cruelty."

"It is none of your business," said the master, insolently.

"You will find that I shall make it my business," said the minister. "And now, boys, be off to your homes, and be here Monday morning at nine o'clock, when this matter shall be gone into."

CHAPTER VI

"ONE THAT RULETH WELL HIS OWN HOUSE"

The news of the school trouble ran through the section like fire through a brule. The younger generations when they heard how Thomas Finch had dared the master, raised him at once to the rank of hero, but the heads of families received the news doubtfully, and wondered what the rising generation was coming to.

The next day Billy Jack heard the story in the Twentieth store, and with some anxiety waited for the news to reach his father's ears, for to tell the truth, Billy Jack, man though he was, held his father in dread.

"How did you come to do it?" he asked Thomas. "Why didn't you let Don begin? It was surely Don's business."

"I don't know. It slipped out," replied Thomas. "I couldn't stand Jimmie's yelling any longer. I didn't know I said anything till I found myself standing up, and after that I didn't seem to care for anything."

"Man! it was fine, though," said Billy Jack. "I didn't think it was in you." And Thomas felt more than repaid for all his cruel beating. It was something to win the approval of Billy Jack in an affair of this kind.

It was at church on the Sabbath day that Donald Finch heard about his son's doings in the school the week before. The minister, in his sermon, thought fit to dwell upon the tendency of the rising generation to revolt against authority in all things, and solemnly laid upon parents the duty and responsibility of seeing to it that they ruled their households well.

It was not just the advice that Donald Finch stood specially in need of, but he was highly pleased with the sermon, and was enlarging upon it in the churchyard where the people gathered between the services, when Peter McRae, thinking that old Donald was hardly taking the minister's advice to himself as he ought, and not knowing that the old man was ignorant of all that had happened in the school, answered him somewhat severely.

"It is good to be approving the sermon, but I would rather be seeing you make a practical application of it."

"Indeed, that is true," replied Donald, "and it would not be amiss for more than me to make application of it."

"Indeed, then, if all reports be true," replied Peter, "it would be well for you to begin at home."

"Mr. McRae," said Donald, earnestly, "it is myself that knows well enough my shortcomings, but if there is any special reason for your remark, I am not aware of it."

This light treatment of what to Peter had seemed a grievous offense against all authority incensed the old dominie beyond all endurance.

"And do you not think that the conduct of your son last week calls for any reproof? And is it you that will stand up and defend it in the face of the minister and his sermon upon it this day?"

Donald gazed at him a few moments as if he had gone mad. At length he replied, slowly, "I do not wish to forget that you are an elder of the church, Mr. McRae, and I will not be charging you with telling lies on me and my family--"

"Tut, tut, man," broke in Long John Cameron, seeing how the matter stood; "he's just referring to yon little difference Thomas had with the master last week. But it's just nothing. Come away in."

"Thomas?" gasped Donald. "My Thomas?"

"You have not heard, then," said Peter, in surprise, and old Donald only shook his head.

"Then it's time you did," replied Peter, severely, "for such things are a disgrace to the community."

"Nonsense!" said Long John. "Not a bit of it! I think none the less of Thomas for it." But in matters of this kind Long John could hardly be counted an authority, for it was not so very long ago since he had been beguiled into an affair at the Scotch River which, while it brought him laurels at the hands of the younger generation, did not add to his reputation with the elders of the church.

It did not help matters much that Murdie Cameron and others of his set proceeded to congratulate old Donald, in their own way, upon his son's achievement, and with all the more fervor that they perceived that it moved the solemn Peter to righteous wrath. From one and another the tale came forth with embellishments, till Donald Finch was reduced to such a state of voiceless rage and humiliation that when, at the sound of the opening psalm the congregation moved into the church for the Gaelic service, the old man departed for his home, trembling, silent, amazed.

How Thomas could have brought this disgrace upon him, he could not imagine. If it had been William John, who, with all his good nature, had a temper brittle enough, he would not have been surprised. And then the minister's sermon, of which he had spoken in such open and enthusiastic approval, how it condemned him for his neglect of duty toward his family, and held up his authority over his household to scorn. It was a terrible blow to his pride.

"It is the Lord's judgment upon me," he said to himself, as he tramped his way through the woods. "It is the curse of Eli that is hanging over me and mine." And with many vows he resolved that, at all costs, he would do his duty in this crisis and bring Thomas to a sense of his sins.

It was in this spirit that he met his family at the supper-table, after their return from the Gaelic service.

"What is this I hear about you, Thomas?" he began, as Thomas came in and took his place at the table. "What is this I hear about you, sir?" he repeated, making a great effort to maintain a calm and judicial tone.

Thomas remained silent, partly because he usually found speech difficult, but chiefly because he dreaded his father's wrath.

"What is this that has become the talk of the countryside and the disgrace of my name?" continued the father, in deepening tones.

"No very great disgrace, surely," said Billy Jack, lightly, hoping to turn his father's anger.

"Be you silent, sir!" commanded the old man, sternly. "I will ask for your opinion when I require it. You and others beside you in this house need to learn your places."

Billy Jack made no reply, fearing to make matters worse, though he found it hard not to resent this taunt, which he knew well was flung at his mother.

"I wonder at you, Thomas, after such a sermon as yon. I wonder you are able to sit there unconcerned at this table. I wonder you are not hiding your head in shame and confusion." The old man was lashing himself into a white rage, while Thomas sat looking stolidly before him, his slow tongue finding no words of defense. And indeed, he had little thought of defending himself. He was conscious of an acute self-condemnation, and yet, struggling through his slow-moving mind there was a feeling that in some sense he could not define, there was justification for what he had done.

"It is not often that Thomas has grieved you," ventured the mother, timidly, for, with all her courage, she feared her husband when he was in this mood.

"Woman, be silent!" blazed forth the old man, as if he had been waiting for her words. "It is not for you to excuse his wickedness. You are too fond of that work, and your children are reaping the fruits of it."

Billy Jack looked up quickly as if to answer, but his mother turned her face full upon him and commanded him with steady eyes, giving, herself, no sign of emotion except for a slight tightening of the lips and a touch of color in her face.

"Your children have well learned their lesson of rebellion and deceit," continued her husband, allowing his passion a free rein. "But I vow unto the Lord I will put an end to it now, whatever. And I will give you to remember, sir," turning to Thomas, "to the end of your days, this occasion. And now, hence from this table. Let me not see your face till the Sabbath is past, and then, if the Lord spares me, I shall deal with you."

Thomas hesitated a moment as if he had not quite taken in his father's words, then, leaving his supper untouched, he rose slowly, and without a word climbed the ladder to the loft. The mother followed him a moment with her eyes, and then once more turning to Billy Jack, held him with calm, steady gaze. Her immediate fear was for her eldest son. Thomas, she knew, would in the mean time simply suffer what might be his lot, but for many a day she had lived in terror of an outbreak between her eldest son and her husband. Again Billy Jack caught her look, and commanded himself to silence.

"The fire is low, William John," she said, in a quiet voice. Billy Jack rose, and from the wood-box behind the stove, replenished the fire, reading perfectly his mother's mind, and resolving at all costs to do her will.

At the taking of the books that night the prayer, which was spoken in a tone of awful and almost inaudible solemnity, was for the most part an exaltation of the majesty and righteousness of the government of God, and a lamentation over the wickedness and rebellion of mankind. And Billy Jack thought it was no good augury that it closed with a petition for grace to maintain the honor of that government, and to uphold that righteous majesty in all the relations of life. It was a woeful evening to them all, and as soon as possible the household went miserably to bed.

Before going to her room the mother slipped up quietly to the loft and found Thomas lying in his bunk, dressed and awake. He was still puzzling out his ethical problem. His conscience clearly condemned him for his fight with the master, and yet, somehow he could not regret having stood up for Jimmie and taken his punishment. He expected no mercy at his father's hands next morning. The punishment he knew would be cruel enough, but it was not the pain that Thomas was dreading; he was dimly struggling with the sense of outrage, for ever since the moment he had stood up and uttered his challenge to the master, he had felt himself to be different. That moment now seemed to belong to the distant years when he was a boy, and now he could not imagine himself submitting to a flogging from any man, and it seemed to him strange and almost impossible that even his father should lift his hand to him.

"You are not sleeping, Thomas," said his mother, going up to his bunk.

"No, mother."

"And you have had no supper at all."

"I don't want any, mother."

The mother sat silent beside him for a time, and then said, quietly, "You did not tell me, Thomas."

"No, mother, I didn't like."

"It would have been better that your father should have heard this from--I mean, should have heard it at home. And--you might have told me, Thomas."

"Yes, mother, I wish now I had. But, indeed, I can't understand how it happened. I don't feel as if it was me at all." And then Thomas told his mother all the tale, finishing his story with the words, "And I couldn't help it, mother, at all."

The mother remained silent for a little, and then, with a little tremor in her voice, she replied: "No, Thomas, I know you couldn't help it, and I--" here her voice quite broke--"I am not ashamed of you."

"Are you not, mother?" said Thomas, sitting up suddenly in great surprise. "Then I don't care. I couldn't make it out well."

"Never you mind, Thomas, it will be well," and she leaned over him and kissed him. Thomas felt her face wet with tears, and his stolid reserve broke down.

"Oh, mother, mother, I don't care now," he cried, his breath coming in great sobs. "I don't care at all." And he put his arms round his mother, clinging to her as if he had been a child.

"I know, laddie, I know," whispered his mother. "Never you fear, never fear." And then, as if to herself, she added, "Thank the Lord you are not a coward, whatever."

Thomas found himself again without words, but he held his mother fast, his big body shaking with his sobs.

"And, Thomas," she continued, after a pause, "your father--we must just be patient." All her life long this had been her struggle. "And--and--he is a good man." Her tears were now flowing fast, and her voice had quite lost its calm.

Thomas was alarmed and distressed. He had never in all his life seen his mother weep, and rarely had heard her voice break.

"Don't, mother," he said, growing suddenly quiet himself. "Don't you mind, mother. It'll be all right, and I'm not afraid."

"Yes," she said, rising and regaining her self-control, "it will be all right, Thomas. You go to sleep." And there were such evident reserves of strength behind her voice that Thomas lay down, certain that all would be well. His mother had never failed him.

The mother went downstairs with the purpose in her heart of having a talk with her husband, but Donald Finch knew her ways well, and had resolved that he would have no speech with her upon the matter, for he knew that it would be impossible for him to persevere in his intention to "deal with" Thomas, if he allowed his wife to have any talk with him.

The morning brought the mother no opportunity of speech with her husband. He, contrary to his custom, remained until breakfast in his room. Outside in the kitchen, he could hear Billy Jack's cheerful tones and hearty laugh, and it angered him to think that his displeasure should have so little effect upon his household. If the house had remained shrouded in gloom, and the family had gone about on tiptoes and with bated breath, it would have shown no more than a proper appreciation of the father's displeasure; but as Billy Jack's cheerful words and laughter fell upon his ear, he renewed his vows to do his duty that day in upholding his authority, and bringing to his son a due sense of his sin.

In grim silence he ate his breakfast, except for a sharp rebuke to Billy Jack, who had been laboring throughout the meal to make cheerful conversation with

Jessac and his mother. At his father's rebuke Billy Jack dropped his cheerful tone, and avoiding his mother's eyes, he assumed at once an attitude of open defiance, his tones and words plainly offering to his father war, if war he would have.

"You will come to me in the room after breakfast," said his father, as Thomas rose to go to the stable.

"There's a meeting of the trustees at nine o'clock at the school- house at which Thomas must be present," interposed Billy Jack, in firm, steady tones.

"He may go when I have done with him," said his father, angrily, "and meantime you will attend to your own business."

"Yes, sir, I will that!" Billy Jack's response came back with fierce promptness.

The old man glanced at him, caught the light in his eyes, hesitated a moment, and then, throwing all restraint to the winds, thundered out, "What do you mean, sir?"

"What I say. I am going to attend to my own business, and that soon." Billy Jack's tone was quick, eager, defiant.

Again the old man hesitated, and then replied, "Go to it, then."

"I am going, and I am going to take Thomas to that meeting at nine o'clock."

"I did not know that you had business there," said the old man, sarcastically.

"Then you may know it now," blazed forth Billy Jack, "for I am going. And as sure as I stand here, I will see that Thomas gets fair play there if he doesn't at home, if I have to lick every trustee in the section."

"Hold your peace, sir!" said his father, coming nearer him. "Do not give me any impertinence, and do not accuse me of unfairness."

"Have you heard Thomas's side of the story?" returned Billy Jack.

"I have heard enough, and more than enough."

"You haven't heard both sides."

"I know the truth of it, whatever, the shameful and disgraceful truth of it. I know that the country-side is ringing with it. I know that in the house of God the minister held up my family to the scorn of the people. And I vowed to do my duty to my house."

The old man's passion had risen to such a height that for a moment Billy Jack quailed before it. In the pause that followed the old man's outburst the mother came to her son.

"Hush, William John! You are not to forget yourself, nor your duty to your father and to me. Thomas will receive full justice in this matter." There was a quiet strength and dignity in her manner that commanded immediate attention from both men.

The mother went on in a low, even voice, "Your father has his duty to perform, and you must not take upon yourself to interfere."

Billy Jack could hardly believe his ears. That his mother should desert him, and should support what he knew she felt to be injustice and tyranny, was more than he could understand. No less perplexed was her husband.

As they stood there looking at each other, uncertain as to the next step, there came a knock at the back door. The mother went to open it, pausing on her way to push back some chairs and put the room to rights, thus allowing the family to regain its composure.

"Good morning, Mrs. Finch. You will be thinking I have slept in your barn all night." It was Long John Cameron.

"Come away in, Mr. Cameron. It is never too early for friends to come to this house," said Mrs. Finch, her voice showing her great relief.

Long John came in, glanced shrewdly about, and greeted Mr. Finch with great heartiness.

"It's a fine winter day, Mr. Finch, but it looks as if we might have a storm. You are busy with the logs, I hear."

Old Donald was slowly recovering himself.

"And a fine lot you are having," continued Long John. "I was just saying the other day that it was wonderful the work you could get through."

"Indeed, it is hard enough to do anything here," said Donald Finch, with some bitterness.

"You may say so," responded Long John, cheerfully. "The snow is that deep in the bush, and--"

"You were wanting to see me, Mr. Cameron," interrupted Donald. "I have a business on hand which requires attention."

"Indeed, and so have I. For it is--"

"And indeed, it is just as well you and all should know it, for my disgrace is well known."

"Disgrace!" exclaimed Long John.

"Ay, disgrace. For is it not a disgrace to have the conduct of your family become the occasion of a sermon on the Lord's Day?"

"Indeed, I did not think much of yon sermon, whatever," replied Long John.

"I cannot agree with you, Mr. Cameron. It was a powerful sermon, and it was only too sorely needed. But I hope it will not be without profit to myself."

"Indeed, it is not the sermon you have much need of," said Long John, "for every one knows what a--"

"Ay, it is myself that needs it, but with the help of the Lord I will be doing my duty this morning."

"And I am very glad to hear that," replied Long John, "for that is why I am come."

"And what may you have to do with it?" asked the old man.

"As to that, indeed," replied Long John, coolly, "I am not yet quite sure. But if I might ask without being too bold, what is the particular duty to which you are referring?"

"You may ask, and you and all have a right to know, for I am about to visit upon my son his sins and shame."

"And is it meaning to wheep him you are?"

"Ay," said the old man, and his lips came fiercely together.

"Indeed, then, you will just do no such thing this morning."

"And by what right do you interfere in my domestic affairs?" demanded old Donald, with dignity. "Answer me that, Mr. Cameron."

"Right or no right," replied Long John, "before any man lays a finger on Thomas there, he will need to begin with myself. And," he added, grimly, "there are not many in the county who would care for that job."

Old Donald Finch looked at his visitor in speechless amazement. At length Long John grew excited.

"Man alive!" he exclaimed, "it's a quare father you are. You may be thinking it disgrace, but the section will be proud that there is a boy in it brave enough to stand up for the weak against a brute bully." And then he proceeded to tell the tale as he had heard it from Don, with such strong passion and such rude vigor, that in spite of himself old Donald found his rage vanish, and his heart began to move within him toward his son.

"And it is for that," cried Long John, dashing his fist into his open palm, "it is for that that you would punish your son. May God forgive me! but the man that lays a finger on Thomas yonder, will come into sore grief this day. Ay, lad," continued Long John, striding toward Thomas and gripping him by the shoulders with both hands, "you are a man, and you stood up for the weak yon day, and if you efer will be wanting a friend, remember John Cameron."

"Well, well, Mr. Cameron," said old Donald, who was more deeply moved than he cared to show, "it maybe as you say. It maybe the lad was not so much in the wrong."

"In the wrong?" roared Long John, blowing his nose hard. "In the wrong? May my boys ever be in the wrong in such a way!"

"Well," said old Donald, "we shall see about this. And if Thomas has suffered injustice it is not his father will refuse to see him righted." And soon they were all off to the meeting at the school- house.

Thomas was the last to leave the room. As usual, he had not been able to find a word, but stood white and trembling, but as he found himself alone with his mother, once more his stolid reserve broke down, and he burst into a strange and broken cry, "Oh, mother, mother," but he could get no further.

"Never mind, laddie," said his mother, "you have borne yourself well, and your mother is proud of you."

At the investigation held in the school-house, it became clear that, though the insubordination of both Jimmie and Thomas was undeniable, the provocation by the master had been very great. And though the minister, who was superintendent of instruction for the district, insisted that the master's authority must, at all costs, be upheld, such was the rage of old Donald Finch and Long John Cameron that the upshot was that the master took his departure from the section, glad enough to escape with bones unbroken.

CHAPTER VII

FOXY

After the expulsion of the master, the Twentieth School fell upon evil days, for the trustees decided that it would be better to try "gurl" teachers, as Hughie contemptuously called them; and this policy prevailed for two or three years, with the result that the big boys left the school, and with their departure the old heroic age passed away, to be succeeded by an age soft, law-abiding, and distinctly commercial.

The spirit of this unheroic age was incarnate in the person of "Foxy" Ross. Foxy got his name, in the first instance, from the peculiar pinky red shade of hair that crowned his white, fat face, but the name stuck to him as appropriately descriptive of his tricks and his manners. His face was large, and smooth, and fat, with wide mouth, and teeth that glistened when he smiled. His smile was like his face, large, and smooth, and fat. His eyes, which were light gray--white, Hughie called them--were shifty, avoiding the gaze that sought to read them, or piercingly keen, according as he might choose.

After the departure of the big boys, Foxy gradually grew in influence until his only rival in the school was Hughie. Foxy's father was the storekeeper in the Twentieth, and this brought within Foxy's reach possibilities of influence that gave him an immense advantage over Hughie. By means of bull's-eyes and "lickerish" sticks, Foxy could win the allegiance of all the smaller boys and many of the bigger ones, while with the girls, both big and small, his willingness to please and his smooth manners won from many affection, and from the rest toleration, although Betsy Dan Campbell asserted that whenever Foxy Ross came near her she felt something creeping up her backbone.

With the teacher, too, Foxy was a great favorite. He gave her worshipful reverence and many gifts from his father's store, eloquent of his devotion. He was never detected in mischief, and was always ready to expose the misdemeanors of the other boys. Thus it came that Foxy was the paramount influence within the school.

Outside, his only rival was Hughie, and at times Hughie's rivalry became dangerous. In all games that called for skill, activity, and reckless daring, Hughie was easily leader. In "Old Sow," "Prisoner's Base," but especially in the ancient and noble game of "Shinny," Hughie shone peerless and supreme. Foxy hated games, and shinny, the joy of those giants of old, who had torn victory from the Sixteenth, and even from the Front one glorious year, was at once Foxy's disgust and terror. As a little boy, he could not for the life of him avoid turning his back to wait shuddering, with humping shoulders, for the enemy's charge, and in anything like a melee, he could not help jumping into the air at every dangerous stroke.

And thus he brought upon himself the contempt even of boys much smaller than himself, who, under the splendid and heroic example of those who led them, had only one ambition, to get a whack at the ball, and this ambition they gratified on every possible occasion reckless of consequences. Hence, when the last of the big boys, Thomas Finch, against whose solid mass hosts had flung themselves to destruction, finally left the school, Foxy, with great skill, managed to divert the energies of the boys to games less violent and dangerous, and by means of his bull's-eyes and his liquorice, and his large, fat smile, he drew after him a very considerable following of both girls and boys.

The most interesting and most successful of Foxy's schemes was the game of "store," which he introduced, Foxy himself being the storekeeper. He had the trader's genius for discovering and catering to the weaknesses of people, and hence his store became, for certain days of the week, the center of life during the recreation hours. The store itself was a somewhat pretentious successor to the little brush cabin with wide open front, where in the old days the boys used to gather, and lying upon piles of fragrant balsam boughs before the big blazing fire placed in front, used to listen to the master talk, and occasionally read.

Foxy's store was built of slabs covered with thick brush, and set off with a plank counter and shelves, whereon were displayed his wares. His stock was never too large for his personal transportation, but its variety was almost infinite, bull's-eyes and liquorice, maple sugar and other "sweeties," were staples. Then, too, there were balls of gum, beautifully clear, which in its raw state Foxy gathered from the ends of the pine logs at the sawmill, and which, by a process of boiling and clarifying known only to himself, he brought to a marvelous perfection.

But Foxy's genius did not confine itself to sweets. He would buy and sell and "swap" anything, but in swapping no bargain was ever completed unless there was money for Foxy in the deal. He had goods second-hand and new, fish-hooks and marbles, pot-metal knives with brass handles, slate-pencils that would "break square," which were greatly desired by all, skate-straps, and buckskin whangs.

But Foxy's financial ability never displayed itself with more brilliancy than when he organized the various games of the school so as to have them begin and end with the store. When the river and pond were covered with clear, black ice, skating would be the rage, and then Foxy's store would be hung with skate-straps, and with cedar-bark torches, which were greatly in demand for the skating parties that thronged the pond at night. There were no torches like Foxy's. The dry cedar bark any one could get from the fences, but Foxy's torches were always well soaked in oil and bound with wire, and were prepared with such excellent skill that they always burned brighter and held together longer than any others. These cedar-bark torches Foxy disposed of to the larger boys who came down to the pond at night. Foxy's methods of finance were undoubtedly marked by ability, and inasmuch as his accounts were never audited, the profits were large and sure. He made it a point to purchase a certain proportion of his supplies from his father, who was proud of his son's financial ability, but whether his purchases always equaled his sales no one ever knew.

If the pond and river were covered with snow, then Foxy would organize a deer-hunt, when all the old pistols in the section would be brought forth, and the store would display a supply of gun caps, by the explosion of which deadly ammunition the deer would be dropped in their tracks, and drawn to the store by prancing steeds whose trappings had been purchased from Foxy.

When the interest in the deer-hunt began to show signs of waning, Foxy would bring forth a supply of gunpowder, for the purchase of which any boy who owned a pistol would be ready to bankrupt himself. In this Hughie took a leading part, although he had to depend upon the generosity of others for the thrilling excitement of bringing down his deer with a pistol-shot, for Hughie had never been able to save coppers enough to purchase a pistol of his own.

But deer-hunting with pistols was forbidden by the teacher from the day when Hughie, in his eagerness to bring his quarry down, left his ramrod in his pistol, and firing at Aleck Dan Campbell at point-blank range, laid him low with a lump on the side of his head as big as a marble. The only thing that saved Aleck's life, the teacher declared, was his thick crop of black hair. Foxy was in great wrath at Hughie for his recklessness, which laid the deer-hunting under the teacher's ban, and which interfered seriously with the profits of the store.

But Foxy was far too great a man to allow himself to be checked by any such misfortune as this. He was far too astute to attempt to defy the teacher and carry on the forbidden game, but with great ability he adapted the principles of deer-hunting to a game even more exciting and profitable. He organized the game of "Injuns," some of the boys being set apart as settlers who were to defend the fort, of which the store was the center, the rest to constitute the invading force of savages.

The result was, that the trade in caps and gunpowder was brisker than ever, for not only was the powder needed for the pistols, but even larger quantities were necessary for the slow-matches which hissed their wrath at the approaching enemy, and the mounted guns, for which earthen ink-bottles did excellently, set out on a big stump to explode, to the destruction of scores of creeping redskins advancing through the bush, who, after being mutilated and mangled by these terrible explosions, were dragged into the camp and scalped. Foxy's success was phenomenal. The few pennies and fewer half-dimes and dimes that the boys had hoarded for many long weeks would soon have been exhausted had

Hughie not wrecked the game.

Hughie alone had no fear of Foxy, but despised him utterly. He had stood and yelled when those heroes of old, Murdie and Don Cameron, Curly Ross, and Ranald Macdonald, and last but not to be despised Thomas Finch, had done battle with the enemy from the Sixteenth or the Front, and he could not bring himself to acknowledge the leadership of Foxy Ross, for all his bull's-eyes and liquorice. Not but what Hughie yearned for bull's-eyes and liquorice with great yearning, but these could not atone to him for the loss out of his life of the stir and rush and daring of the old fighting days. And it galled him that the boys of the Sixteenth could flout the boys of the Twentieth in all places and on all occasions with impunity.

But above all, it seemed to him a standing disgrace that the habitant teamsters from the north, who in former days found it a necessary and wise precaution to put their horses to a gallop as they passed the school, in order to escape with sleighs intact from the hordes that lined the roadway, now drove slowly past the very gate without an apparent tremor. But besides all this, he had an instinctive shrinking from Foxy, and sympathized with Betsy Dan in her creepy feeling whenever he approached. Hence he refused allegiance, and drew upon himself Foxy's jealous hatred.

It was one of Foxy's few errors in judgment that, from his desire to humiliate Hughie and to bring him to a proper state of subjection, he succeeded in shutting him out from the leadership in the game of "Injuns," for Hughie promptly refused a subordinate position and withdrew, like Achilles, to his tent. But, unlike Achilles, though he sulked, he sulked actively, and to some purpose, for, drawing off with him his two faithful henchmen, "Fusie"--neither Hughie nor any one else ever knew another name for the little French boy who had drifted into the settlement and made his home with the MacLeods--and Davie "Scotch," a cousin of Davie MacDougall, newly arrived from Scotland, he placed them in positions which commanded the store entrance, and waited until the settlers had all departed upon their expedition against the invading Indians. Foxy, with one or two smaller boys, was left in charge of the store waiting for trade.

In a few moments Foxy's head appeared at the door, when, whiz! a snowball skinned his ear and flattened itself with a bang against the slabs.

"Hold on there! Stop that! You're too close up," shouted Foxy, thinking that the invaders were breaking the rules of the game.

Bang! a snowball from another quarter caught him fair in the neck.

"Here, you fools, you! Stop that!" cried Foxy, turning in the direction whence the snowball came and dodging round to the side of the store. But this was Hughie's point of attack, and soon Foxy found that the only place of refuge was inside, whither he fled, closing the door after him. Immediately the door became a target for the hidden foe.

Meantime, the Indian war was progressing, but now and again a settler would return to the fort for ammunition, and the moment he reached the door a volley of snowballs would catch him and hasten his entrance. Once in it was dangerous to come out.

By degrees Hughie augmented his besieging force from the more adventurous settlers and Indians, and placed them in the bush surrounding the door.

The war game was demoralized, but the new game proved so much more interesting that it was taken up with enthusiasm and prosecuted with vigor. It was rare sport. For the whole noon hour Hughie and his bombarding force kept Foxy and his friends in close confinement, from which they were relieved only by the ringing of the school bell, for at the sound of the bell Hughie and his men, having had their game, fled from Foxy's wrath to the shelter of the school.

When Foxy appeared it was discovered that one eye was half shut, but the light that gleamed from the other was sufficiently baleful to give token of the wrath blazing within, and Hughie was not a little anxious to know what form Foxy's vengeance would take. But to his surprise, by the time recess had come Foxy's wrath had apparently vanished, and he was willing to treat Hughie's exploit in the light of a joke. The truth was, Foxy never allowed passion to interfere with business, and hence he resolved that he must swallow his rage, for he realized clearly that Hughie was far too dangerous as a foe, and that he might become exceedingly valuable as an ally. Within a week Hughie was Foxy's partner in business, enjoying hugely the privilege of dispensing the store goods, with certain perquisites that naturally attached to him as storekeeper.

CHAPTER VIII

FOXY'S PARTNER

It was an evil day for Hughie when he made friends with Foxy and became his partner in the store business, for Hughie's hoardings were never large, and after buying a Christmas present for his mother, according to his unfailing custom, they were reduced to a very few pennies indeed. The opportunities for investment in his new position were many and alluring. But all Hughie's soul went out in longing for a pistol which Foxy had among his goods, and which would fire not only caps, but powder and ball, and his longing was sensibly increased by Foxy generously allowing him to try the pistol, first at a mark, which Hughie hit, and then at a red squirrel, which he missed. By day Hughie yearned for this pistol, by night he dreamed of it, but how he might secure it for his own he did not know.

Upon this point he felt he could not consult his mother, his usual counselor, for he had an instinctive feeling that she would not approve of his having a pistol in his possession; and as for his father, Hughie knew he would soon make "short work of any such folly." What would a child like Hughie do with a pistol? He had never had a pistol in all his life. It was difficult for the minister to realize that young Canada was a new type, and he would have been more than surprised had any one told him that already Hughie, although only twelve, was an expert with a gun, having for many a Saturday during the long, sunny fall roamed the woods, at first in company with Don, and afterwards with Don's gun alone, or followed by Fusie or Davie Scotch. There was thus no help for Hughie at home. The price of the pistol reduced to the lowest possible sum, was two dollars and a half, which Foxy declared was only half what he would charge any one else but his partner.

"How much have you got altogether?" he asked Hughie one day, when Hughie was groaning over his poverty.

"Six pennies and two dimes," was Hughie's disconsolate reply. He had often counted them over. "Of course," he went on, "there's my XL knife. That's worth a lot, only the point of the big blade's broken."

"Huh!" grunted Foxy, "there's jist the stub left."

"It's not!" said Hughie, indignantly. "It's more than half, then. And it's bully good stuff, too. It'll nick any knife in the school"; and Hughie dived into his pocket and pulled out his knife with a handful of boy's treasures.

"Hullo!" said Foxy, snatching a half-dollar from Hughie's hand, "whose is that?"

"Here, you, give me that! That's not mine," cried Hughie.

"Whose is it, then?"

"I don't know. I guess it's mother's. I found it on the kitchen floor, and I know it's mother's."

"How do you know?"

"I know well enough. She often puts money on the window, and it fell down. Give me that, I tell you!" Hughie's eyes were blazing dangerously, and Foxy handed back the half-dollar.

"O, all right. You're a pretty big fool," he said, indifferently. "'Losers seekers, finders keepers.' That's my rule."

Hughie was silent, holding his precious half-dollar in his hand, deep in his pocket.

"Say," said Foxy, changing the subject, "I guess you had better pay up for your powder and caps you've been firing."

"I haven't been firing much," said Hughie, confidently.

"Well, you've been firing pretty steady for three weeks."

"Three weeks! It isn't three weeks."

"It is. There's this week, and last week when the ink-bottle bust too soon and burnt Fusie's eyebrows, and the week before when you shot Aleck Dan, and it was the week before that you began, and that'll make it four."

"How much?" asked Hughie, desperately, resolved to know the worst.

Foxy had been preparing for this. He took down a slate-pencil box with a sliding lid, and drew out a bundle of crumbled slips which Hughie, with sinking heart, recognized as his own vouchers.

"Sixteen pennies." Foxy had taken care of this part of the business.

"Sixteen!" exclaimed Hughie, snatching up the bunch.

"Count them yourself," said Foxy, calmly, knowing well he could count on Hughie's honesty.

"Seventeen," said Hughie, hopelessly.

"But one of those I didn't count," said Foxy, generously. "That's the one I gave you to try at the first. Now, I tell you," went on Foxy, insinuatingly, "you have got how much at home?" he inquired.

"Six pennies and two dimes." Hughie's tone indicated despair.

"You've got six pennies and two dimes. Six pennies and two dimes. That's twenty--that's thirty-two cents. Now if you paid me that thirty-two cents, and if you could get a half-dollar anywhere, that would be eighty-two. I tell you what I would do. I would let you have that pistol for only one dollar more. That ain't much," he said.

"Only a dollar more," said Hughie, calculating rapidly. "But where would I get the fifty cents?" The dollar seemed at that moment to Hughie quite a possible thing, if only the fifty cents could be got. The dollar was more remote, and therefore less pressing.

Foxy had an inspiration.

"I tell you what. You borrow that fifty cents you found, and then you can pay me eighty-two cents, and--and--" he hesitated--"perhaps you will find some more, or something."

Hughie's eyes were blazing with great fierceness.

Foxy hastened to add, "And I'll let you have the pistol right off, and you'll pay me again some time when you can, the other dollar."

Hughie checked the indignant answer that was at his lips. To have the pistol as his own, to take home with him at night, and to keep all Saturday--the temptation was great, and coming suddenly upon Hughie, was too much for him. He would surely, somehow, soon pay back the fifty cents, he argued, and Foxy would wait for the dollar. And yet that half-dollar was not his, but his mother's, and more than that, if he asked her for it, he was pretty sure she would refuse. But then, he doubted his mother's judgment as to his ability to use firearms, and besides, this pistol at that price was a great bargain, and any of the boys might pick it up. Poor Hughie! He did not know how ancient was that argument, nor how frequently it had done duty in smoothing the descent to the lower regions. The pistol was good to look at, the opportunity of securing it was such as might not occur again, and as for the half- dollar, there could be no harm in borrowing that for a little while.

That was Foxy's day of triumph, but to Hughie it was the beginning of many woeful days and nights. And his misery came upon him swift and sure, in the very moment that he turned in from the road at the manse gate, for he knew that at the end of the lane would be his mother, and his winged feet, upon which he usually flew from the gate home, dragged heavily.

He found his mother, not at the door, but in the large, pleasant living-room, which did for all kinds of rooms in the manse. It was dining-room and sewing-room, nursery and playroom, but it was always a good room to enter, and in spite of playthings strewn about, or snippings of cloth, or other stour, it was always a place of brightness and of peace, for it was there the mother was most frequently to be found. This evening she was at the sewing-machine busy with Hughie's Sunday clothes, with the baby asleep in the cradle beside her in spite of the din of the flying wheels, and little Robbie helping to pull through the long seam. Hughie shrank from the warm, bright, loving atmosphere that seemed to fill the room, hating to go in, but in a moment he realized that he must "make believe" with his mother, and the pain of it and the shame of it startled and amazed him. He was glad that his mother did not notice him enter, and by the time he had put away his books he had braced himself to meet her bright smile and her welcome kiss.

The mother did not apparently notice his hesitation.

"Well, my boy, home again?" she cried, holding out her hand to him with the air of good comradeship she always wore with him. "Are you very hungry?"

"You bet!" said Hughie, kissing her, and glad of the chance to get away.

"Well, you will find something pretty nice in the pantry we saved for you. Guess what."

"Don't know."

"I know," shouted Robbie. "Pie! It's muzzie's pie. Muzzie tept it for 'oo."

"Now, Robbie, you were not to tell," said his mother, shaking her finger at him.

"O-o-o, I fordot," said Robbie, horrified at his failure to keep his promise.

"Never mind. That's a lesson you will have to learn many times, how to keep those little lips shut. And the pie will be just as good."

"Thank you, mother," said Hughie. "But I don't want your pie."

"My pie!" said the mother. "Pie isn't good for old women."

"Old women!" said Hughie, indignantly. "You're the youngest and prettiest woman in the congregation," he cried, and forgetting for the moment his sense of meanness, he threw his arms round his mother.

"Oh, Hughie, shame on you! What a dreadful flatterer you are!" said his mother. "Now, run away to your pie, and then to your evening work, my boy, and we will have a good lesson together after supper."

Hughie ran away, glad to get out of her presence, and seizing the pie, carried it out to the barn and hurled it far into the snow. He felt sure that a single bite of it would choke him.

If he could only have seen Foxy any time for the next hour, how gladly would he have given him back his pistol, but by the time he had fed his cow and the horses, split the wood and carried it in, and prepared kindling for the morning's fires, he had become accustomed to his new self, and had learned his first lesson in keeping his emotions out of his face. But from that night, and through all the long weeks of the breaking winter, when games in the woods were impossible by reason of the snow and water, and when the roads were deep with mud, Hughie carried his burden with him, till life was one long weariness and dread.

And through these days he was Foxy's slave. A pistol without ammunition was quite useless. Foxy's stock was near at hand. It was easy to write a voucher for a penny's worth of powder or caps, and consequently the pile in Foxy's pencil-box steadily mounted till Hughie was afraid to look at it. His chance of being free from his own conscience was still remote enough.

During these days, too, Foxy reveled in his power over his rival, and ground his slave in bitter bondage, subjecting him to such humiliation as made the school wonder and Hughie writhe; and if ever Hughie showed any sign of resentment or rebellion, Foxy could tame him to groveling submission by a single word. "Well, I guess I'll go down to-night to see your mother," was all he needed to say to make Hughie grovel again. For with Hughie it was not the fear of his father's wrath and heavy punishment, though that was terrible enough, but the dread that his mother should know, that made him grovel before his tyrant, and wake at night in a cold sweat. His mother's tender anxiety for his pale face and gloomy looks only added to the misery of his heart.

He had no one in whom he could confide. He could not tell any of the boys, for he was unwilling to lose their esteem, besides, it was none of their business; he was terrified of his father's wrath, and from his mother, his usual and unfailing resort in every trouble of his whole life, he was now separated by his terrible secret.

Then Foxy began to insist upon payment of his debts. Spring was at hand, the store would soon be closed up, for business was slack in the summer, and besides, Foxy had other use for his money.

"Haven't you got any money at all in your house?" Foxy sneered one day, when Hughie was declaring his inability to meet his debts.

"Of course we have," cried Hughie, indignantly.

"Don't believe it," said Foxy, contemptuously.

"Father's drawer is sometimes full of dimes and half-dimes. At least, there's an awful lot on Mondays, from the collections, you know," said Hughie.

"Well, then, you had better get some for me, somehow," said Foxy. "You might borrow some from the drawer for a little while."

"That would be stealing," said Hughie.

"You wouldn't mean to keep it," said Foxy. "You would only take it for a while. It would just be borrowing."

"It wouldn't," said Hughie, firmly. "It's taking out of his drawer. It's stealing, and I won't steal."

"Huh! you're mighty good all at once. What about that half- dollar?"

"You said yourself that wasn't stealing," said Hughie, passionately.

"Well, what's the difference? You said it was your mother's, and this is your father's. It's all the same, except that you're afraid to take your father's."

"I'm not afraid. At least it isn't that. But it's different to take money out of a drawer, that isn't your own."

"Huh! Mighty lot of difference! Money's money, wherever it is. Besides, if you borrowed this from your father, you could pay back your mother and me. You would pay the whole thing right off."

Once more Hughie argued with himself. To be free from Foxy's hateful tyranny, and to be clear again with his mother--for that he would be willing to suffer almost anything. But to take money out of that drawer was awfully like stealing. Of course he would pay it back, and after all it would only be borrowing. Besides, it would enable him to repay what he owed to his mother and to Foxy. Through all the mazes of specious argument Hughie worked his way, arriving at no conclusion, except that he carried with him a feeling that if he could by some means get that money out of the drawer in a way that would not be stealing, it would be a vast relief, greater than words could tell.

That night brought him the opportunity. His father and mother were away at the prayer meeting. There was only Jessie left in the house, and she was busy with the younger children. With the firm resolve that he would not take a single half-dime from his father's drawer, he went into the study. He would like to see if the drawer were open. Yes, it was open, and the Sabbath's collection lay there with all its shining invitation. He tried making up the dollar and a half out of the dimes and half-dimes. What a lot of half-dimes it took! But when he used the quarters and dimes, how much smaller the piles were. Only two quarters and five dimes made up the dollar, and the pile in the drawer looked pretty much the same as before. Another quarter-dollar withdrawn from the drawer made little difference. He looked at the little heaps on the table. He believed he could make Foxy take that for his whole debt, though he was sure he owed him more. Perhaps he had better make certain. He transferred two more dimes and a half-dime from the drawer to the table. It was an insignificant little heap. That would certainly clear off his whole indebtedness and make him a free man.

He slipped the little heaps of money from the table into his pocket, and then suddenly he realized that he had never decided to take the money. The last resolve he could remember making was simply to see how the dollar and a half looked. Without noticing, he had passed the point of final decision. Alas! like many another, Hughie found the going easy and the slipping smooth upon the down incline. Unconsciously he had slipped into being a thief.

Now he could not go back. His absorbing purpose was concealment. Quietly shutting the drawer, he was slipping hurriedly up to his own room, when on the stairway he met Jessie.

"What are you doing here, Jessie?" he asked, sharply.

"Putting Robbie off to bed," said Jessie, in surprise. "What's the matter with you?"

"What's the matter?" echoed Hughie, smitten with horrible fear that perhaps she knew. "I just wanted to know," he said, weakly.

He slipped past her, holding his pocket tight lest the coins should rattle. When he reached his room he stood listening in the dark to Jessie going down the stairs. He was sure she suspected something. He would go back and put the money in the drawer again, whenever she reached the kitchen. He stood there with his heart-beats filling his ears, waiting for the kitchen door to slam.

Then he resolved he would wrap the money up in paper and put it safely away, and go down and see if Jessie knew. He found one of his old copybooks, and began tearing out a leaf. What a noise it made! Robbie would surely wake up, and then Jessie would come back with the light. He put the copy-book under the quilt, and holding it down firmly with one hand, removed the leaf with the other. With great care he wrapped up the dimes and half-dimes by themselves. They fitted better together. Then he took up the quarters, and was proceeding to fold them in a similar parcel, when he heard Jessie's voice from below.

"Hughie, what are you doing?" She was coming up the stair.

He jumped from the bed to go to meet her. A quarter fell on the floor and rolled under the bed. It seemed to Hughie as if it would never stop rolling, and as if Jessie must hear it. Wildly he scrambled on the floor in the dark, seeking for the quarter, while Jessie came nearer and nearer.

"Are you going to bed already, Hughie?" she asked.

Quickly Hughie went out to the hall to meet her.

"Yes," he yawned, gratefully seizing upon her suggestion. "I'm awfully sleepy. Give me the candle, Jessie," he said, snatching it from her hand. "I want to go downstairs."

"Hughie, you are very rude. What would your mother say? Let me have the candle immediately, I want to get Robbie's stockings."

Hughie's heart stood still.

"I'll throw them down, Jessie. I want the candle downstairs just a minute."

"Leave that candle with me," insisted Jessie. "There's another on the dining-room table you can get."

"I'll not be a minute," said Hughie, hurrying downstairs. "You come down, Jessie, I want to ask you something. I'll throw you Robbie's stockings."

"Come back here, the rude boy that you are," said Jessie, crossly, "and bring me that candle."

There was no reply. Hughie was standing, pale and shaking, in the dining-room, listening intently for Jessie's step. Would she go into his room, or would she come down? Every moment increased the agony of his fear.

At length, with a happy inspiration, he went to the cupboard, opened the door noisily, and began rattling the dishes.

"Mercy me!" he heard Jessie exclaim at the top of the stair. "That boy will be my death. Hughie," she called, "just shut that cupboard! You know your mother doesn't like you to go in there."

"I only want a little," called out Hughie, still moving the dishes, and hearing, to his great relief, Jessie's descending step. In desperation he seized a dish of black currant preserves which he found on the cupboard shelf, and spilled it over the dishes and upon the floor just as Jessie entered the room.

"Land sakes alive, boy! Will you never be done your mischief?" she cried, rushing toward him.

"Oh!" he said, "I spilt it."

"Spilt it!" echoed Jessie, indignantly, "you needn't be telling me that. Bring me a cloth from the kitchen."

"I don't know where it is, Jessie," cried Hughie, slipping upstairs again with his candle.

To his great relief he saw that Jessie's attention was so entirely taken up with removing the stains of the preserves from the cupboard shelves and dishes, that she for the moment forgot everything else, Robbie's stockings included.

Hurrying to his room, and shading the candle with his hand lest the light should waken his little brother, he hastily seized the money upon the bed quilt, and after a few moments' searching under the bed, found the strayed quarter.

With these in his hand he passed into his mother's room. Leaving the candle there, he came back to the head of the stairs and listened for a moment, with great satisfaction, to Jessie muttering to herself while she cleaned up the mess he had made. Then he turned, and with trembling fingers he swiftly made up the quarter- dollars into another parcel. With a great sigh of relief he put the two parcels in his pocket, and seizing his candle turned to leave the room. As he did so, he caught sight of himself in the glass. With a great shock of surprise he stood gazing at the terrified, white face, with the staring eyes.

"What a fool I am!" he said, looking at himself in the glass. "Nobody will know, and I'll pay this back soon."

His eyes wandered to a picture which stood on a little shelf beside the glass. It was a picture of his mother, the one he loved best of all he had ever seen of her.

There was a sudden stab of pain at his heart, his breath came in a great sob. For a moment he looked into the eyes that looked back at him so full of love and reproach.

"I won't do it," he said, grinding his teeth hard, and forthwith turned to go to his father's study.

But as he left the room he saw Jessie half-way up the stairs.

"What are you doing now?" she cried, wrathfully. "Up to some mischief, I doubt."

With a sudden, inexplicable rage, Hughie turned toward her.

"It's none of your business! You mind your own business, will you, and leave me alone." The terrible emotions of the last few minutes were at the back of his rage.

"Just wait, you," said Jessie, "till your mother comes. Then you'll hear it."

"You shut your mouth!" cried Hughie, his passion sweeping his whole being like a tempest. "You shut your mouth, you old cat, or I'll throw this candle at you." He raised the candle high in his hand as he spoke, and altogether looked so desperate that Jessie stood in terror lest he should make good his threat.

"Stop, now, Hughie," she entreated. "You will be setting the house on fire."

Hughie hesitated a moment, and then turned from her, and going into his room, banged the door in her face, and Jessie, not knowing what to make of it all, went slowly downstairs again, forgetting once more Robbie's stockings.

"The old cat!" said Hughie to himself. "She just stopped me. I was going to put it back."

The memory that he had resolved to undo his wrong brought him a curious sense of relief.

"I was just going to put it back," he said, "when she had to interfere."

He was conscious of a sense of injury against Jessie. It was not his fault that that money was not now in the drawer.

"I'll put it back in the morning, anyhow," he said, firmly. But even as he spoke he was conscious of an infinality in his determination, while he refused to acknowledge to himself a secret purpose to leave the question open till the morning. But this determination, inconclusive though it was, brought him a certain calm of mind, so that when his mother came into his room she found him sound asleep.

She stood beside his bed looking down upon him for a few moments, with face full of anxious sadness.

"There's something wrong with the boy," she said to herself, stooping to kiss him. "There's something wrong with him," she repeated, as she left the room. "He's not the same."

During these weeks she had been conscious that Hughie had changed in some way to her. The old, full, frank confidence was gone. There was a constraint in his manner she could not explain. "He is no longer a child," she would say to herself, seeking to allay the pain in her heart. "A boy must have his secrets. It is foolish in me to think anything else. Besides, he is not well. He is growing too fast." And indeed, Hughie's pale, miserable face gave ground enough for this opinion.

"That boy is not well," she said to her husband.

"Which boy?"

"Hughie," she replied. "He is looking miserable, and somehow he is different."

"Oh, nonsense! He eats well enough, and sleeps well enough," said her husband, making light of her fears.

"There's something wrong," repeated his wife. "And he hates his school."

"Well, I don't wonder at that," said her husband, sharply. "I don't see how any boy of spirit could take much pleasure in that kind of a school. The boys are just wasting their time, and worse than that, they have lost all the old spirit. I must see to it that the policy of those close-fisted trustees is changed. I am not going to put up with those chits of girls teaching any longer."

"There may be something in what you say," said his wife, sadly, "but certainly Hughie is always begging to stay at home from school."

"And indeed, he might as well stay home," answered her husband, "for all the good he gets."

"I do wish we had a good man in charge," replied his wife, with a great sigh. "It is very important that these boys should have a good, strong man over them. How much it means to a boy at Hughie's time of life! But so few are willing to come away into the backwoods here for so small a salary."

Suddenly her husband laid down his pipe.

"I have it!" he exclaimed. "The very thing! Wouldn't this be the very thing for young Craven. You remember, the young man that Professor MacLauchlan was writing about."

His wife shook her head very decidedly.

"Not at all," she said. "Didn't Professor MacLauchlan say he was dissipated?"

"O, just a little wild. Got going with some loose companions. Out here there would be no temptation."

"I am not at all sure of that," said his wife, "and I would not like Hughie to be under his influence."

"MacLauchlan says he is a young man of fine disposition and of fine parts," argued her husband, "and if temptation were removed from him he believes he would turn out a good man."

Mrs. Murray shook her head doubtfully. "He is not the man to put Hughie under just now."

"What are we to do with Hughie?" replied her husband. "He is getting no good in the school as it is, and we cannot send him away yet."

"Send him away!" exclaimed his wife. "No, no, not a child like that."

"Craven might be a very good man," continued her husband. "He might perhaps live with us. I know you have more than enough to do now," he added, answering her look of dismay, "but he would be a great help to Hughie with his lessons, and might start him in his classics. And then, who knows what you might make of the young man."

Mrs. Murray did not respond to her husband's smile, but only replied, "I am sure I wish I knew what is the matter with the boy, and I wish he could leave school for a while."

"O, the boy is all right," said her husband, impatiently. "Only a little less noisy, as far as I can see."

"No, he is not the same," replied his wife. "He is different to me." There was almost a cry of pain in her voice.

"Now, now, don't imagine things. Boys are full of notions at Hughie's age. He may need a change, but that is all."

With this the mother tried to quiet the tumult of anxious fear and pain she found rising in her heart, but long after the house was still, and while both her boy and his father lay asleep, she kept pouring forth that ancient sacrifice of self-effacing love before the feet of God.

CHAPTER IX

HUGHIE'S EMANCIPATION

Hughie rose late next morning, and the hurry and rush of getting off to school in time left him no opportunity to get rid of the little packages in his pocket, that seemed to burn and sting him through his clothes. He determined to keep them safe in his pocket all day and put them back in the drawer at night. His mother's face, white with her long watching, and sad and anxious in spite of its brave smile, filled him with such an agony of remorse that, hurrying through his breakfast, he snatched a farewell kiss, and then tore away down the lane lest he should be forced to confess all his terrible secret.

The first person who met him in the school-yard was Foxy.

"Have you got that?" was his salutation.

A sudden fury possessed Hughie.

"Yes, you red-headed, sneaking fox," he answered, "and I hope it will bring you the curse of luck, anyway."

Foxy hurried him cautiously behind the school, with difficulty concealing his delight while Hughie unrolled his little bundles and counted out the quarters and dimes and half dimes into his hand.

"There's a dollar, and there's a quarter, and--and--there's another," he added, desperately, "and God may kill me on the spot if I give you any more!"

"All right, Hughie," said Foxy, soothingly, putting the money into his pocket. "You needn't be so mad about it. You bought the pistol and the rest right enough, didn't you?"

"I know I did, but--but you made me, you big, sneaking thief--and then you--" Hughie's voice broke in his rage. His face was pale, and his black eyes were glittering with fierce fury, and in his heart he was conscious of a wild longing to fall upon Foxy and tear him to pieces. And Foxy, big and tall as he was, glanced at Hughie's face, and saying not a word, turned and fled to the front of the school where the other boys were.

Hughie followed slowly, his heart still swelling with furious rage, and full of an eager desire to be at Foxy's smiling, fat face.

At the school door stood Miss Morrison, the teacher, smiling down upon Foxy, who was looking up at her with an expression of such sweet innocence that Hughie groaned out between his clenched teeth, "Oh, you red-headed devil, you! Some day I'll make you smile out of the other side of your big, fat mouth."

'Who are you swearing at?" It was Fusie.

"Oh, Fusie," cried Hughie, "let's get Davie and get into the woods. I'm not going in to-day. I hate the beastly place, and the whole gang of them."

Fusie, the little, harum-scarum French waif was ready for anything in the way of adventure. To him anything was better than the even monotony of the school routine. True, it might mean a whipping both from the teacher and from Mrs. McLeod; but as to the teacher's whipping, Fusie was prepared to stand that for a free day in the woods, and as to the other, Fusie declared that Mrs. McLeod's whipping "wouldn't hurt a skeeter."

To Davie Scotch, however, playing truant was a serious matter. He had been reared in an atmosphere of reverence for established law and order, but when Hughie gave command, to Davie there seemed nothing for it but to obey.

The three boys watched till the school was called, and then crawling along on their stomachs behind the heavy cedar-log fence, they slipped into the balsam thicket at the edge of the woods and were safe. Here they flung down their schoolbags, and lying prone upon the fragrant bed of pine-needles strewn thickly upon the moss, they peered out through the balsam boughs at the house of their bondage with an exultant sense of freedom and a feeling of pity, if not of contempt, for the unhappy and spiritless creatures who were content to be penned inside any house on such a day as this, and with such a world outside.

For some minutes they rolled about upon the soft moss and balsam- needles and the brown leaves of last year, till their hearts were running over with a deep and satisfying delight. It is hard to resist the ministry of the woods. The sympathetic silence of the trees, the aromatic airs that breathe through the shady spaces, the soft mingling of broken lights--these all combine to lay upon the spirit a soothing balm, and bring to the heart peace. And Hughie, sensitive at every pore to that soothing ministry, before long forgot for a time even Foxy, with his fat, white face and smiling mouth, and lying on the broad of his back, and looking up at the far-away blue sky through the interlacing branches and leaves, he began to feel again that it was good to be alive, and that with all his misery there were compensations.

But any lengthened period of peaceful calm is not for boys of the age and spirit of Hughie and his companions.

"What are you going to do?" asked Fusie, the man of adventure.

"Do nothing," said Hughie from his supine position. "This is good enough for me."

"Not me," said Fusie, starting to climb a tall, lithe birch, while Hughie lazily watched him. Soon Fusie was at the top of the birch, which began to sway dangerously.

"Try to fly into that balsam," cried Hughie.

"No, sir!"

"Yes, go on."

"Can't do it."

"Oh, pshaw! you can."

"No, nor you either. That's a mighty big jump."

"Come on down, then, and let me try," said Hughie, in scorn. His laziness was gone in the presence of a possible achievement.

In a few minutes he had taken Fusie's place a the top of the swaying birch. It did not look so easy from the top of the birch as from the ground to swing into the balsam-tree. However, he could not go back now.

"Dinna try it, Hughie!" cried Davie to him. "Ye'll no mak it, and ye'll come an awfu' cropper, as sure as deith." But Hughie, swaying gently back and forth, was measuring the distance of his drop. It was not a feat so very difficult, but it called for good judgment and steady nerve. A moment too soon or a moment too late in letting go, would mean a nasty fall of twenty feet or more upon the solid ground, and one never knew just how one would light.

"I wudna dae it, Hughie," urged Davie, anxiously.

But Hughie, swaying high in the birch, heeded not the warning, and suddenly swinging out from the slender trunk and holding by his hands, he described a parabola, and releasing the birch dropped on to the balsam top. But balsam-trees are of uncertain fiber, and not to be relied upon, and this particular balsam, breaking off short in Hughie's hands, allowed him to go crashing through the branches to the earth.

"Man! man!" cried Davie Scotch, bending over Hughie as he lay white and still upon the ground. "Are ye deid? Maircy me! he's deid," sobbed Davie, wringing his hands. "Fusie, Fusie, ye gowk! where are ye gone?"

In a moment or two Fusie reappeared through the branches with a capful of water, and dashed it into Hughie's face, with the result that the lad opened his eyes, and after a gasp or two, sat up and looked about him.

"Och, laddie, laddie, are ye no deid?" said Davie Scotch.

"What's the matter with you, Scottie?" asked Hughie, with a bewildered look about him. "And who's been throwing water all over me?" he added, wrathfully, as full consciousness returned.

"Man! I'm glad to see ye mad. Gang on wi' ye," shouted Davie, joyously. "Ye were deid the noo. Ay, clean deid. Was he no, Fusie?" Fusie nodded.

"I guess not," said Hughie. "It was that rotten balsam top," looking vengefully at the broken tree.

"Lie doon, man," said Davie, still anxiously hovering about him. "Dinna rise yet awhile."

"Oh, pshaw!" said Hughie, and he struggled to his feet; "I'm all right." But as he spoke he sank down upon the moss, saying, "I feel kind of queer, though."

"Lie still, then, will ye," said Davie, angrily. "Ye're fair obstinate."

"Get me some water, Fusie," said Hughie, rather weakly.

"Run, Fusie, ye gomeril, ye!"

In a minute Fusie was back with a capful of water.

"That's better. I'm all right now," said Hughie, sitting up.

"Hear him!" said Davie. "Lie ye doon there, or I'll gie ye a crack that'll mak ye glad tae keep still."

For half an hour the boys lay on the moss discussing the accident fully in all its varying aspects and possibilities, till the sound of wheels came up the road.

"Who's that, Fusie?" asked Hughie, lazily.

"Dunno me," said Fusie, peering through the trees.

"Do you, Scotty?"

"No, not I."

Hughie crawled over to the edge of the brush.

"Why, you idiots! it's Thomas Finch. Thomas!" he called, but Thomas drove straight on. In a moment Hughie sprang up, forgetting all about his weakness, and ran out to the roadside.

"Hello, Thomas!" he cried, waving his hand. Thomas saw him, stopped, and looked at him, doubtfully. He, with all the Section, knew how the school was going, and he easily guessed what took Hughie there.

"I'm not going to school to-day," said Hughie, answering Thomas's look.

Thomas nodded, and sat silent, waiting. He was not a man to waste his words.

"I hate the whole thing!" exclaimed Hughie.

"Foxy, eh?" said Thomas, to whom on other occasions Hughie had confided his grievances, and especially those he suffered at the hands of Foxy.

"Yes, Foxy," cried Hughie, in a sudden rage. "He's a fat-faced sneak! And the teacher just makes me sick!"

Thomas still waited.

"She just smiles and smiles at him, and he smiles at her. Ugh! I can't stand him."

"Not much harm in smiling," said Thomas, solemnly.

"Oh, Thomas, I hate the school. I'm not going to go any more."

Thomas looked gravely down upon Hughie's passionate face for a few moments, and then said, "You will do what your mother wants you, I guess."

Hughie said nothing in reply, while Thomas sat pondering.

Finally he said, with a sudden inspiration, "Hughie, come along with me, and help me with the potatoes."

"They won't let me," grumbled Hughie. "At least father won't. I don't like to ask mother."

Thomas's eyes opened in surprise. This was a new thing in Hughie.

"I'll ask your mother," he said, at length. "Get in with me here."

Still Hughie hesitated. To get away from school was joy enough, to go with Thomas to the potato planting was more than could be hoped for. But still he stood making pictures in the dust with his bare toes.

"There's Fusie," he said, "and Davie Scotch."

"Well," said Thomas, catching sight of those worthies through the trees, "let them come, too."

Fusie was promptly willing, but Davie was doubtful. He certainly would not go to the manse, where he might meet the minister, and meeting the minister's wife under the present circumstances was a little worse.

"Well, you can wait at the gate with Fusie," suggested Hughie, and so the matter was settled.

Fortunately for Hughie, his father was not at home. But not Thomas's earnest entreaties nor Hughie's eager pleading would have availed with the mother, for attendance at school was a sacred duty in her eyes, had it not been that her boy's face, paler than usual, and with the dawning of a new defiance in it, startled her, and confirmed in her the fear that all was not well with him.

"Well, Thomas, he may go with you to the Cameron's for the potatoes, but as to going with you to the planting, that is another thing. Your mother is not fit to be troubled with another boy, and especially a boy like Hughie. And how is she to-day, Thomas?" continued Mrs. Murray, as Thomas stood in dull silence before her.

"She's better," said Thomas, answering more quickly than usual, and with a certain eagerness in his voice. "She's a great deal better, and Hughie will do her no harm, but good."

Mrs. Murray looked at Thomas as he spoke, wondering at the change in his voice and manner. The heavy, stolid face had changed since she had last seen it. It was finer, keener, than before. The eyes, so often dull, were lighted up with a new, strange fire.

"She's much better," said Thomas again, as if insisting against Mrs. Murray's unbelief.

"I am glad to hear it, Thomas," she said, gently. "She will soon be quite well again, I hope, for she has had a long, long time of suffering."

"Yes, a long, long time," replied Thomas. His face was pale, and in his eyes was a look of pain, almost of fear.

"And you will come to see her soon?" he added. There was almost a piteous entreaty in his tone.

"Yes, Thomas, surely next week. And meantime, I shall let Hughie go with you."

A look of such utter devotion poured itself into Thomas's eyes that Mrs. Murray was greatly moved, and putting her hand on his shoulder, she said, gently, "'He will give His angels charge.' Don't be afraid, Thomas."

"Afraid!" said Thomas, with a kind of gasp, his face going white. "Afraid! No. Why?" But Mrs. Murray turned from him to hide the tears that she could not keep out of her eyes, for she knew what was before Thomas and them all.

Meantime Hughie was busy putting into his little carpet-bag what he considered the necessary equipment for his visit.

"You must wear your shoes, Hughie."

"Oh, mother, shoes are such an awful bother planting potatoes. They get full of ground and everything."

"Well, put them in your bag, at any rate, and your stockings, too. You may need them."

By degrees Hughie's very moderate necessities were satisfied, and with a hurried farewell to his mother he went off with Thomas. At the gate they picked up Fusie and Davie Scotch, and went off to the Cameron's for the seed potatoes, Hughie's heart lighter than it had been for many a day. And all through the afternoon, and as he drove home with Thomas on the loaded bags, his heart kept singing back to the birds in the trees overhead.

It was late in the afternoon when they drove into the yard, for the roads were still bad in the swamp, where the corduroy had been broken up by the spring floods.

Thomas hurried through unhitching, and without waiting to unharness he stood the horses in their stalls, saying, "We may need them this afternoon again," and took Hughie off to the house straight-way.

The usual beautiful order pervaded the house and its surroundings. The back yard, through which the boys came from the barn, was free of litter; the chips were raked into neat little piles close to the wood-pile, for summer use. On a bench beside the "stoop" door was a row of milk-pans, lapping each other like scales on a fish, glittering in the sun. The large summer kitchen, with its spotless floor and white-washed walls, stood with both its doors open to the sweet air that came in from the fields above, and was as pleasant a room to look in upon as one could desire. On the sill of the open window stood a sweet-scented geranium and a tall fuschia with white and crimson blossoms hanging in clusters. Bunches of wild flowers stood on the table, on the dresser, and up beside the clock, and the whole room breathed of sweet scents of fields and flowers, and "the name of the chamber was peace."

Beside the open window sat the little mother in an arm-chair, the embodiment of all the peaceful beauty and sweet fragrance of the room.

"Well, mother," said Thomas, crossing the floor to her and laying his hand upon her shoulder, "have I been long away? I have brought Hughie back with me, you see."

"Not so very long, Thomas," said the mother, her dark face lighting with a look of love as she glanced up at her big son. "And I am glad to see Hughie. He will excuse me from rising," she added, with fine courtesy.

Hughie hurried toward her.

"Yes, indeed, Mrs. Finch. Don't think of rising." But he could get no further. Boy as he was, and at the age when boys are most heartless and regardless, he found it hard to keep his lip and his voice steady and to swallow the lump in his throat, and in spite of all he could do his eyes were filling up with tears as he looked into the little woman's face, so worn and weary, so pathetically bright.

It was months since he had seen her, and during these months a great change had come to her and to the Finch household. After suffering long in secret, the mother had been forced to confess to a severe pain in her breast and under her arm. Upon examination the doctor pronounced the case to be malignant cancer, and there was nothing for it but removal. It was what Dr. Grant called "a very beautiful operation, indeed," and now she was recovering her strength, but only slowly, so slowly that Thomas at times found his heart sink with a vague fear. But it was not the pain of the wound that had wrought that sweet, pathetic look into the little woman's face, but the deeper pain she carried in her heart for those she loved better than herself.

The mother's sickness brought many changes into the household, but the most striking of all the changes was that wrought in the slow and stolid Thomas. The father and Billy Jack were busy with the farm matters outside, upon little Jessac, now a girl of twelve years, fell the care of the house, but it was Thomas that, with the assistance of a neighbor at first, but afterwards alone, waited on his mother, dressing the wound and nursing her. These weeks of watching and nursing had wrought in him the subtle change that stirred Mrs. Murray's heart as she looked at him that day, and that made even Hughie wonder. For one thing his tongue was loosed, and Thomas talked to his mother of all that he had seen and heard on the way to the Cameron's and back, making much of his little visit to the manse, and of Mrs. Murray's kindness, and enlarging upon her promised visit, and all with such brightness and picturesqueness of speech that Hughie listened amazed. For all the years he had known Thomas he had never heard from his lips so many words as in the last few minutes of talk with his mother. Then, too, Thomas seemed to have found his fingers, for no woman could have arranged more deftly and with gentler touch the cushions at his mother's back, and no nurse could have measured out the medicine and prepared her egg-nog with greater skill. Hughie could hardly believe his eyes and ears. Was this Thomas the stolid, the clumsy, the heavy- handed, this big fellow with the quick tongue and the clever, gentle hand?

Meantime Jessac had set upon the table a large pitcher of rich milk, with oat cakes and butter, and honey in the comb.

"Now, Hughie, lad, draw in and help yourself. You and Thomas will be too hungry to wait for supper," said the mother. And Hughie, protesting politely that he was not very hungry, proceeded to establish the contrary, to the great satisfaction of himself and the others.

"Now, Thomas," said the mother, "we had better cut the seed."

"Indeed, and not a seed will you cut, mother," said Thomas, emphatically. "You may boss the job, though. I'll bring the potatoes to the back door." And this he did, thinking it no trouble to hitch up the team to draw the wagon into the back yard so that his mother might have a part in the cutting of the seed potatoes, as she had had every year of her life on the farm.

Very carefully, and in spite of her protests that she could walk quite well, Thomas carried his mother out to her chair in the shade of the house, arranging with tender solicitude the pillows at her back and the rug at her feet. Then they set to work at the potatoes.

"Mind you have two eyes in every seed, Hughie," said Jessac, severely.

"Huh! I know. I've cut them often enough," replied Hughie, scornfully.

"Well, look at that one, now," said Jessac, picking up a seed that Hughie had let fall; "that's only got one eye."

"There's two," said Hughie, triumphantly.

"That's not an eye," said Jessac, pointing to a mark on the potato; "that's where the top grew out of, isn't it, mother?"

"It is, isn't it?" appealed Hughie.

Mrs. Finch took the seed and looked at it.

"Well, there's one very good eye, and that will do."

"But isn't that the mark of the top, mother?" insisted Jessac. But the mother only shook her head at her.

"That's right, Jessac," said Thomas, driving off with his team; "you look after Hughie, and mother will look after you both till I get back, and there'll be a grand crop this year."

It was a happy hour for them all. The slanting rays of the afternoon sun filled the air with a genial warmth. A little breeze bore from the orchard near by a fragrance of apple-blossoms. A matronly hen, tethered by the leg to her coop, raised indignant protest against the outrage on her personal liberty, or clucked and crooned her invitations, counsels, warnings, and encouragements, in as many different tones, to her independent, fluffy brood of chicks, while a huge gobbler strutted up and down, thrilling with pride in the glossy magnificence of his outspread tail and pompous, mighty chest.

Hughie was conscious of a deep and grateful content, but across his content lay a shadow. If only that would lift! As he watched Thomas with his mother, he realized how far he had drifted from his own mother, and he thought with regret of the happy days, which now seemed so far in the past, when his mother had shared his every secret. But for him those days could never come again.

At supper, Hughie was aware of some subtle difference in the spirit of the home. As to Thomas so to his father a change had come. The old man was as silent as ever, indeed more so, but there was no asperity in his silence. His critical, captious manner was gone. His silence was that of a great sorrow, and of a great fear. While there was more cheerful conversation than ever at the table, there was through all a new respect and a certain tender consideration shown toward the silent old man at the head, and all joined in an effort to draw him from his gloom. The past months of his wife's suffering had bowed him as with the weight of years. Even Hughie could note this.

After supper the old man "took the Books" as usual, but when, as High Priest, he "ascended the Mount of Ordinances to offer the evening sacrifice," he was as a man walking in thick darkness bewildered and afraid. The prayer was largely a meditation on the heinousness of sin and the righteous judgments of God, and closed with an exaltation of the Cross, with an appeal that the innocent might be spared the punishment of the guilty. The conviction had settled in the old man's mind that "the Lord was visiting upon him and his family his sins, his pride, his censoriousness, his hardness of heart." The words of his prayer fell meaningless upon Hughie's English ears, but the boy's heart quivered in response to the agony of entreaty in the pleading tones, and he rose from his knees awed and subdued.

There was no word spoken for some moments after the prayer. With people like the Finches it was considered to be an insult to the Almighty to depart from "the Presence" with any unseemly haste. Then Thomas came to help his mother to her room, but she, with her eyes upon her husband, quietly put Thomas aside and said, "Donald, will you tak me ben?"

Rarely had she called him by his name before the family, and all felt that this was a most unusual demonstration of tenderness on her part.

The old man glanced quickly at her from under his overhanging eyebrows, and met her bright upward look with an involuntary shake of the head and a slight sigh. Comfort was not for him, and he must not delude himself. But with a little laugh she put her hand on his arm, and as if administering reproof to a little child, she said some words in Gaelic.

"Oh, woman, woman!" said Donald in reply, "if it was yourself we had to deal with--"

"Whisht, man! Will you be putting me before your Father in heaven?" she said, as they disappeared into the other room.

There was no fiddle that evening. There was no heart for it with Thomas, neither was there time, for there was the milking to do, and the "sorting" of the pails and pans, and the preparing for churning in the morning, so that when all was done, the long evening had faded into the twilight and it was time for bed.

Before going upstairs, Thomas took Hughie into "the room" where his mother's bed had been placed. Thomas gave her her medicine and made her comfortable for the night.

"Is there nothing else now, mother?" he said, still lingering about her.

"No, Thomas, my man. How are the cows doing?"

"Grand; Blossom filled a pail to-night, and Spotty almost twice. She's a great milker, yon."

"Yes, and so was her mother. I remember she used to fill two pails when the grass was good."

"I remember her, too. Her horns curled right back, didn't they? And she always looked so fierce."

"Yes, but she was a kindly cow. And will the churn be ready for the morning?"

"Yes, mother, we'll have buttermilk for our porridge, sure enough."

"Well, you'll need to be up early for that, too early, Thomas, lad, for a boy like you."

"A boy like me!" said Thomas, feigning indignation, and stretching himself to his full height. "Where would you be getting your men, mother?"

"You are man enough, laddie," said his mother, "and a good one you will come to be, I doubt. And you, too, Hughie, lad," she added, turning to him. "You will be like your father."

"I dunno," said Hughie, his face flushing scarlet. He was weary and sick of his secret, and the sight of the loving comradeship between Thomas and his mother made his burden all the heavier.

"What's wrong with yon laddie?" asked Mrs. Finch, when Hughie had gone away to bed.

"Now, mother, you're too sharp altogether. And how do you know anything is wrong with him?"

"I warrant you his mother sees it. Something is on his mind. Hughie is not the lad he used to be. He will not look at you straight, and that is not like Hughie."

"Oh, mother, you're a sharp one," said Thomas. "I thought no one had seen that but myself. Yes, there is something wrong with him. It's something in the school. It's a poor place nowadays, anyway, and I wish Hughie were done with it."

"He must keep at the school, Thomas, and I only wish you could do the same." His mother sighed. She had her own secret ambition for Thomas, and though she never opened her heart to her son, or indeed to any one, Thomas somehow knew that it was her heart's desire to see him "in the pulpit."

"Never you mind, mother," he said, brightly. "It'll all come right. Aren't you always the one preaching faith to me?"

"Yes, laddie, and it is needed, and sorely at times."

"Now, mither," said Thomas, dropping into her native speech, "ye mauna be fashin' yersel. Ye'll jist say 'Now I lay me,' and gang to sleep like a bairnie."

"Ay, that's a guid word, laddie, an' a'll tak it. Ye may kiss me guid nicht. A'll tak it."

Thomas bent over her and whispered in her ear, "Ay, mither, mither, ye're an angel, and that ye are."

"Hoots, laddie, gang awa wi' ye," said his mother, but she held her arms about his neck and kissed him once and again. There was no one to see, and why should they not give and take their heart's fill of love.

But when Thomas stood outside the room door, he folded his arms tight across his breast and whispered with lips that quivered, "Ay, mither, mither, mither, there's nane like ye. There's nane like ye." And he was glad that when he went upstairs, he found Hughie unwilling to talk.

The next three days they were all busy with the planting of the potatoes, and nothing could have been better for Hughie. The sweet, sunny air, and the kindly, wholesome earth and honest hard work were life and health to mind and heart and body. It is wonderful how the touch of the kindly mother earth cleanses the soul from its unwholesome humors. The hours that Hughie spent in working with the clean, red earth seemed somehow to breathe virtue into him. He remembered the past months like a bad dream. They seemed to him a hideous unreality, and he could not think of Foxy and his schemes, nor of his own weakness in yielding to temptation, without a horrible self-loathing. He became aware of a strange feeling of sympathy and kinship with old Donald Finch. He seemed to understand his gloom. During those days their work brought those two together, for Billy Jack had the running of the drills, and to Thomas was intrusted the responsibility of "dropping" the potatoes, so Hughie and the old man undertook to "cover" after Thomas.

Side by side they hoed together, speaking not a word for an hour at a time, but before long the old man appeared to feel the lad's sympathy. Hughie was quick to save him steps, and eager in many ways to anticipate his wishes. He was quick, too, with the hoe, and ambitious to do his full share of the work, and this won the old man's respect, so that by the end of the first day there was established between them a solid basis of friendship.

Old Donald Finch was no cheerful companion for Hughie, but it was to Hughie a relief, more than anything else, that he was not much with either Thomas or Billy Jack.

"You're tired," he ventured, in answer to a deep sigh from the old man, toward the close of the day.

"No, laddie," replied the old man, "I know not that I am working. The burden of toil is the least of all our burdens." And then, after a pause, he added, "It is a terrible thing, is sin."

To an equal in age the old man would never have ventured this confidence, but to Hughie, to his own surprise, he found it easy to talk.

"A terrible thing," he repeated, "and it will always be finding you out."

Hughie listened to him with a fearful sinking of heart, thinking of himself and his sin.

"Yes," repeated the old man, with awful solemnity, "it will come up with you at last."

"But," ventured Hughie, timidly, "won't God forgive? Won't he ever forget?"

The old man looked at him, leaning upon his hoe.

"Yes, he will forgive. But for those who have had great privileges, and who have sinned against light--I will not say."

The fear deepened in Hughie's heart.

"Do you mean that God will not forgive a man who has had a good chance, an elder, or a minister, or--or--a minister's son, say, like me?"

There was something in Hughie's tone that startled the old man. He glanced at Hughie's face.

"What am I saying?" he cried. "It is of myself I am thinking, boy, and of no minister or minister's son."

But Hughie stood looking at him, his face showing his terrible anxiety. God and sin were vivid realities to him.

"Yes, yes," said the old man to himself, "it is a great gospel. 'As far as the east is distant from the west.' 'And plenteous redemption is ever found with him.'"

"But, do you think," said Hughie, in a low voice, "God will tell all our sins? Will he make them known?"

"God forbid!" cried the old man. "'And their sins and their iniquities will I remember no more.' 'The depths of the sea.' No, no, boy, he will surely forget, and he will not be proclaiming them."

It was a strange picture. The old man leaning upon the top of his hoe looking over at the lad, the gloom of his face irradiated with a momentary gleam of hope, and the boy looking back at him with almost breathless eagerness.

"It would be great," said Hughie, at last, "if he would forget."

"Yes," said the old man, the gleam in his face growing brighter, "'If we confess our sins he is faithful and just to forgive us,' and forgiving with him is forgetting. Ah, yes, it is a great gospel," he continued, and standing there he lifted up his hand and broke into a kind of chant in Gaelic, of which Hughie could catch no meaning, but the exalted look on the old man's face was translation enough.

"Must we always tell?" said Hughie, after the old man had ceased.

"What are you saying, laddie?"

"I say must we always tell our sins--I mean to people?"

The old man thought a moment. "It is not always good to be talking about our sins to people. That is for God to hear. But we must be ready to make right what is wrong."

"Yes, yes," said Hughie, eagerly, "of course one would be glad to do that."

The old man gave him one keen glance, and began hoeing again.

"Ye'd better be asking ye're mother about that. She will know."

"No, no," said Hughie, "I can't."

The old man paused in his work, looked at the boy for a moment or two, and then went on working again.

"Speak to my woman," he said, after a few strokes of his hoe. "She's a wonderful wise woman." And Hughie wished that he dared.

During the days of the planting they became great friends, and to their mutual good. The mother's keen eyes noted the change both in Hughie and in her husband, and was glad for it. It was she that suggested to Billy Jack that he needed help in the back pasture with the stones. Billy Jack, quick to take her meaning, eagerly insisted that help he must have, indeed he could not get on with the plowing unless the stones were taken off. And so it came that Hughie and the old man, with old Fly hitched up in the stone-boat, spent two happy and not unprofitable days in the back pasture. Gravely they discussed the high themes of God's sovereignty and man's freedom, with all their practical issues upon conduct and destiny. Only once, and that very shyly, did the old man bring round the talk to the subject of their first conversation that meant so much to them both.

"The Lord will not be wanting to shame us beyond what is necessary," he said. "There are certain sins which he will bring to light, but there are those that, in his mercy, he permits us to hide; provided always," he added, with emphasis, "we are done with them."

"Yes, indeed," assented Hughie, eagerly, "and who wouldn't be done with them?"

But the old man shook his head sadly.

"If that were always true a man would soon be rid of his evil heart. But," he continued, as if eager to turn the conversation, "you will be talking with my woman about it. She's a wonderful wise woman, yon."

Somehow the opportunity came to Hughie to take the old man's advice. On Saturday evening, just before leaving for home, he found himself alone with Mrs. Finch sitting beside the open window, watching the sun go down behind the trees.

"What a splendid sunset!" he cried. He was ever sensitive to the majestic drama of nature.

"Ay," said Mrs. Finch, "the clouds and the sun make wonderful beauty together, but without the sun the clouds are ugly things.

Hughie quickly took her meaning.

"They are not pleasant," he said.

"No, not pleasant," she replied, "but with the sunlight upon them they are wonderful."

Hughie was silent for some moments, and then suddenly burst out, "Mrs. Finch, does God forget sins, and will he keep them hid, from people, I mean?"

"Ay," she said, with quiet conviction, "he will forget, and he will hide them. Why should he lay the burden of our sins upon others? And if he does not why should we?"

"Do you mean we need not always tell? I'd like to tell my--some one."

"Ay," she replied, "it's a weary wark and a lanely to carry it oor lane, but it's an awfu' grief to hear o' anither's sin. An awfu' grief," she repeated to herself.

"But," burst out Hughie, "I'll never be right till I tell my mother."

"Ay, and then it is she would be carrying the weight o' it."

"But it's against her," said Hughie, his hands going up to his face. "Oh, Mrs. Finch, it's just awful mean. I don't know how I did it."

"Ye can tell me, laddie, if ye will," said she, kindly, and Hughie poured forth the whole burden that had lain so long upon him, but he told it laying upon Foxy small blame, for during those days, his own part had come to bulk so large with him that Foxy's was almost forgotten.

For some moments after he had done Mrs. Finch sat in silence, leaning forward and patting the boy's bowed head.

"Ay, but he is rightly named," she said, at length.

"Who?" asked Hughie, surprised.

"Yon store-keepin' chiel." Then she added, "But ye're done wi' him and his tricks, and ye'll stand up against him and be a man for the wee laddies."

"Oh, I don't know," said Hughie, too sick at heart and too penetrated with the miserable sense of his own meanness and cowardice, to make any promise.

"And as tae ye're mither, laddie," went on Mrs. Finch, "it will be a sair burden for her." When Mrs. Finch was greatly moved she always dropped into her broadest Scotch.

"Oh, yes, I know," said Hughie, his voice now broken with sobs, "and that's the worst of it. If I didn't have to tell her! She'll just break her heart, I know. She thinks I'm so--oh, oh--" The long pent up feelings came flooding forth in groans and sobs.

For some moments Mrs. Finch sat quietly, and then she said, "Listen, laddie. There is Another to be thought of first."

"Another?" asked Hughie. "Oh, yes, I know. But He knows already, and indeed I have often told Him. But besides, you say He will forget, and take it away. But mother doesn't know, and doesn't suspect."

"Well, then, laddie," said Mrs. Finch, with quiet firmness, "let her tell ye what to do. Mak ye're offer to tell her, and warn her that it'll grieve ye baith, and then let her say."

"Yes, I'll do it. I'll do it to-night, and if she says so, then I'll tell her."

And so he did, and when he came back to the Finch's on Monday morning, for his mother saw that leaving school for a time would be no serious loss, and a week or two with the Finches might be a great gain, he came radiant to Mrs. Finch, and finding her in her chair by the open window alone, he burst forth, "I told her, and she wouldn't let me. She didn't want to know so long as I said it was all made right. And she promised she would trust me just the same. Oh, she's splendid, my mother! And she's coming this week to see you. And I tell you I just feel like--like anything! I can't keep still. I'm like Fido when he's let off his chain. He just goes wild."

Then, after a pause, he added, in a graver tone, "And mother read Zaccheus to me. And isn't it fine how He never said a word to him?"--Hughie was too excited to be coherent--"but stood up for him, and"--here Hughie's voice became more grave--"I'm going to restore fourfold. I'm going to work at the hay, and I fired that old pistol into the pond, and I'm not afraid of Foxy any more, not a bit."

Hughie rushed breathlessly through his story, while the dark face before him glowed with intelligent sympathy, but she only said, when he had done, "It is a graund thing to be free, is it no'?"

CHAPTER X

THE BEAR HUNT

"Is Don round, Mrs. Cameron?"

"Mercy me, Hughie! Did ye sleep in the woods? Come away in. Ye're a sight for sore eyes. Come away in. And how's ye're mother and all?"

"All right, thank you. Is Don in?"

"Don? He's somewhere about the barn. But come away, man, there's a bit bannock here, and some honey."

"I'm in a hurry, Mrs. Cameron, and I can't very well wait," said Hughie, trying to preserve an evenness of tone and not allow his excitement to appear.

"Well, well! What's the matter, whatever?" When Hughie refused a "bit bannock" and honey, something must be seriously wrong.

"Nothing at all, but I'm just wanting Don for a--for something."

"Well, well, just go to the old barn and cry at him."

Hughie found Don in the old barn, busy "rigging up" his plow, for the harvest was in and the fall plowing was soon to begin.

"Man, Don!" cried Hughie, in a subdued voice, "it's the greatest thing you ever heard!"

"What is it now, Hughie? You look fairly lifted. Have you seen a ghost?"

"A ghost? No, something better than that, I can tell you."

Hughie drew near and lowered his voice, while Don worked on indifferently.

"It's a bear, Don."

Don dropped his plow. His indifference vanished. The Camerons were great hunters, and many a bear had they, with their famous black dogs, brought home in their day, but not for the past year or two; and never had Don bagged anything bigger than a fox or a coon.

"Where did you see him?"

"I didn't see him." Don looked disgusted. "But he was in our house last night."

"Look here now, stop that!" said Don, gripping Hughie by the jacket and shaking him.

But Hughie's summer in the harvest-field had built up his muscles, and so he shook himself free from Don's grasp, and said, "Look out there! I'm telling you the truth. Last night father was out late and the supper things were left on the table--some honey and stuff-- and after father had been asleep for a while he was wakened by some one tramping about the house. He got up, came out of his room, and called out, 'Jessie, where are the matches?' And just then there was an awful crash, and something hairy brushed past his leg in the dark and got out of the door. We all came down, and there was the table upset, the dishes all on the floor, and four great, big, deep scratches in the table."

"Pshaw! It must have been Fido."

"Fido was in the barn, and just mad to get out; and besides, the tracks are there yet behind the house. It was a bear, sure enough, and I'm going after him."

"You?"

"Yes, and I want you to come with the dogs."

"Oh, pshaw! Dear knows where he'll be now," said Don, considering.

"Like enough in the Big Swamp or in McLeod's beech bush. They're awful fond of beechnuts. But the dogs can track him, can't they?"

"By jingo! I'd like to get him," said Don, kindling under Hughie's excitement. "Wait a bit now. Don't say a word. If Murdie hears he'll want to come, sure, and we don't want him. You wait here till I get the gun and the dogs."

"Have you got any bullets or slugs?"

"Yes, lots. Why? Have you a gun?"

"Yes, you just bet! I've got our gun. What did you think I was going to do? Put salt on his tail? I've got it down the lane."

"All right, you wait there for me."

"Don't be long," said Hughie, slipping away.

It was half an hour before Don appeared with the gun and the dogs.

"What in the world kept you? I thought you were never coming," said Hughie, impatiently.

"I tell you it's no easy thing to get away with mother on hand, but it's all right. Here's your bullets and slugs. I've brought some bannocks and cheese. We don't know when we'll get home. We'll pick up the track in your brule. Does any one know you're going?"

"No, only Fusie. He wanted to come, but I wouldn't have it. Fusie gets so excited." Hughie's calmness was not phenomenal. He could hardly stand still for two consecutive seconds.

"Well, let's go," and Don set off on a trot, with one of the black dogs in leash and the other following, and after him came Hughie running lightly.

In twenty minutes they were at the manse clearing.

"Now," said Don, pulling up, "where did you say you saw his track?"

"Just back of the house there, and round the barn, and then straight for the brule."

The boys stood looking across the fallen timber toward the barn.

"There's Fido barking," said Hughie. "I bet he's on the scent now."

"Yes," answered Don, "and there's your father, too."

"Gimmini crickets! so it is," said Hughie, slowly. "I don't think it's worth while going up there to get that track. Can't we get it just as well in the woods here?" There were always things to do about the house, and besides, the minister knew nothing of Hughie's familiarity with the gun, and hence would soon have put a stop to any such rash venture as bear-hunting.

The boys waited, listening to Fido, who was running back and forward between the brule and the house barking furiously. The minister seemed interested in Fido's manoeuvres, and followed him a little way.

"Man!" said Hughie, in a whisper, "perhaps he'll go and look for the gun himself. And Fido will find us, sure. I say, let's go."

"Let's wait a minute," said Don, "to see what direction Fido takes, and then we'll put our dogs on."

In a few minutes Hughie breathed more freely, for his father seemed to lose his interest in Fido, and returned slowly to the house.

"Now," said Hughie, "let's get down into the brule as near Fido as we can get."

Cautiously the boys made their way through the fallen timber, keeping as much as possible under cover of the underbrush. But though they hunted about for some time, the dogs evidently got no scent, for they remained quite uninterested in the proceedings.

"We'll have to get up closer to where Fido is," said Don, "and the sooner we get there the better."

"I suppose so," said Hughie. "I suppose I had better go. Fido will stop barking for me." So, while Don lay hid with the dogs in the brule, Hughie stole nearer and nearer to Fido, who was still chasing down toward the brule and back to the house, as if urging some one to come forth and investigate the strange scent he had discovered. Gradually Hughie worked his way closer to Fido until within calling distance.

Just as he was about to whistle for the dog, the back door opened and forth came the minister again. By this time Fido had passed into the brule a little way, and could not be seen from the house. It was an anxious moment for Hughie. He made a sudden desperate resolve. He must secure Fido now, or else give up the chance of getting on the trail of the bear. So he left his place of hiding, and bending low, ran swiftly forward until Fido caught sight of him, and hearing his voice, came to him, barking loudly and making every demonstration of excitement and joy. He seized the dog by the collar and dragged him down, and after holding him quiet for a moment, hauled him back to Don.

"We'll have to take him with us," he said. "I'll put this string on his collar, and he'll go all right." And to this Don agreed, though very unwillingly, for he had no confidence in Fido's hunting ability.

"I tell you he's a great fighter," said Hughie, "if we should ever get near that bear."

"Oh, pshaw!" said Don, "he may fight dogs well enough, but when it comes to a bear, it's a different thing. Every dog is scared of a bear the first time he sees him."

"Well, I bet you Fido won't run from anything," said Hughie, confidently.

To their great relief they saw the minister set off in the opposite direction across the fields.

"Thank goodness! He's off to the McRae's," said Hughie.

"Now, then," said Don, "we'll go back to the track there, and put the dogs on. You go on with Fido." And Hughie set off with Fido pulling eagerly upon the string.

When they reached the spot where Fido had been seized by Hughie, suddenly the black dog who had been following Don at some distance, stopped short and began to growl. In a moment his mate threw up his nose and began sniffing about, the hair rising stiff upon his back.

"He's catching it," said Don, in an excited tone. "Here, you hold him. I must get the other one, or he'll be off." He was not a minute too soon, for the other dog, who had been ranging about, suddenly found the trail, and with a fierce, short bark, was about to dash off when Don threw himself upon him. In a few moments both dogs were on the leash, and set off upon the scent at a great pace. The trail was evidently plain enough to the dogs, for they followed hard, leading the boys deeper and deeper into the bush.

"He's making for the Big Swamp," said Don, and on they went, with eyes and ears on the alert, expecting every moment to hear the snort of a bear, or to meet him on the further side of every bunch of underbrush.

For an hour they went on at a steady trot, over and under fallen logs, splashing through water holes, crashing over dead brushwood, and tearing through the interlacing boughs of the thick underbrush of spruce and balsam. The black dogs never hesitated. They knew well what was their business there, and that they kept strictly in mind. Fido, on the other hand, who loved to roam the woods in an aimless hunt for any and every wild thing that might cross his nose, but who never had seriously hunted anything in particular, trotted good-naturedly behind Hughie with rather a bored expression on his face.

The trail, which had led them steadily north, all at once turned west and away from the swamp.

"Say," said Don, "he's making for Alan Gorrach's cabin."

"Man!" said Hughie, "that would be fine, to get him there. It's good and open, too."

"Too open by a long way," grunted Don. "We'd never get him there."

Sure enough, the dogs led up from the swamp and along the path to Alan's cabin. The door stood open, and in answer to Don's "Horo!" Alan came out.

"What now?" he said, glowering at Don.

"You won't be wanting any dogs to-day, Alan?" said Don, politely.

Alan glanced at him suspiciously, but said not a word.

"These are very good dogs, indeed, Alan."

"Go on your ways, now," said Alan.

"These black ones are not in very good condition, but Fido there is a good, fat dog."

Alan's wrath began to rise.

"Will you be going on, now, about your business?"

"Better take them, Alan, there's a hard winter coming on."

"Mac an' Diabhoil!" cried Alan, in a shrill voice, suddenly bursting into fury. "I will be having your heart's blood," he cried, rushing into his cabin.

"Come on, Hughie," cried Don, and away they rushed, following the black dogs upon the trail of the bear.

Deeper and deeper into the swamp the dogs led the way, the going becoming more difficult and the underbrush thicker at every step. After an hour or two of hard work, the dogs began to falter, and ran hither and thither, now on one scent and then on another, till tired out and disgusted, Don held them in, and threw himself down upon the soft moss that lay deep over everything.

"We're on his old tracks here," said Don, savagely, "and you can't pick out the new from the old."

"His hole must be somewhere not too far away," said Hughie.

"Yes, perhaps it is, but then again it may be across the ridge. At any rate, we'll have some grub."

As they ate the bannocks and cheese, they pictured to themselves what they should do if they ever should come up with the bear.

"One thing we've got to be careful of," said Don, "and that is, not to lose our heads."

"That's so," assented Hughie, feeling quite cool and self-possessed at the time.

"Because if you lose your head you're done for," continued Don. "Remember Ken McGregor?"

"No," said Hughie.

"Didn't you ever hear that? Why, he ran into a bear, and made a drive at him with his axe, but the bear, with one paw knocked the axe clear out of his hand, and with one sweep of the other tore his insides right out. They're mighty cute, too," went on Don. "They'll pretend to be almost dead just to coax you near enough, and then they'll spin round on their hind legs like a rooster. If they ever do catch you, the only thing to do is to lie still and make believe you're dead, and then, unless they're very hungry, they won't hurt you much."

After half an hour's rest, the hunting instinct awoke again within them, and the boys determined to make another attempt. After circling about the swamp for some time, the boys came upon a beaten track which led straight through the heart of the swamp.

"I say," said Don, "this is going to strike the ridge somewhere just about there," pointing northeast, "and if we don't see anything between here and the ridge, we'll strike home that way. It'll be better walking than this cursed swamp, anyway. Are you tired?"

Hughie refused to acknowledge any weariness.

"Well, then, I am," said Don.

The trail was clear enough, and they were able to follow at a good pace, so that in a few minutes, as they had expected, they struck the northeast end of the swamp. Here again they called a halt, and tying up the dogs, lay down upon the dry, brown leaves, lazily eating the beechnuts and discussing their prospects of meeting the bear, and their plans for dealing with him.

"Well, let's go on," at length said Don. "There's just a chance of our meeting him on this ridge. He's got a den somewhere down in the swamp, and he may be coming home this way. Besides, it'll take us all our time, now, to get home before dark. I guess there's no use keeping the dogs any longer. We'll just let them go." So saying, Don let the black dogs go free, but after a little skirmishing through the open beech woods, the dogs appeared to lose all interest in the expedition, and kept close to Don's heels.

Fido, on the other hand, followed, ranging the woods on either side, cheerfully interested in scaring up rabbits, ground-hogs, and squirrels. He had never known the rapture of bringing down big game, and so was content with whatever came his way.

At length the hunters reached the main trail where their paths separated; but a little of the swamp still remained, and on the other side was the open clearing.

"This is your best way," said Don, pointing out the path to Hughie. "We had bad luck to-day, but we'll try again. We may meet him still, you know, so don't fire at any squirrel or anything. If I hear a shot I'll come to you, and you do the same by me."

"I say," said Hughie, "where does this track of mine come out? Is it below the Deepole there, or is it on the other side of the clearing?"

"Why, don't you know?" said Don. "This runs right up to the back of the Fisher's berry patch, and through the sugar-bush to your own clearing. I'll go with you if you like."

"Oh, pshaw!" said Hughie, "I'll find it all right. Come on, Fido." But Fido had disappeared. "Good night, Don."

"Good night," said Don. "Mind you don't fire unless it's at a bear. I'll do the same."

In a few minutes Hughie found himself alone in the thick underbrush of the swamp. The shadows were lying heavy, and the sunlight that still caught the tops of the tall trees was quite lost in the gloom of the low underbrush. Deep moss under foot, with fallen trees and thick-growing balsam and cedars, made the walking difficult, and every step Hughie wished himself out in the clearing. He began to feel, too, the oppression of the falling darkness. He tried whistling to keep up his courage, but the sound seemed to fill the whole woods about him, and he soon gave it up.

After a few minutes he stood still and called for Fido, but the dog had gone on some hunt of his own, and with a sense of deeper loneliness, he set himself again to his struggle with the moss and brush and fallen trees. At length he reached firmer ground, and began with more cheerful heart to climb up to the open.

Suddenly he heard a rustle, and saw the brush in front of him move.

"Oh, there you are, you brute," he cried, "come in here. Come in, Fido. Here, sir!"

He pushed the bushes aside, and his heart jumped and filled his mouth. A huge, black shape stood right across his path not ten paces away. A moment they gazed at each other, and then, with a low growl, the bear began to sway awkwardly toward him. Hughie threw up his gun and fired. The bear paused, snapping viciously and tearing at his wounded shoulder, and then rushed on Hughie without waiting to rise on his hind legs.

Like a flash Hughie dodged behind the brush, and then fled like the wind toward the open. Looking over his shoulder, he saw the bear shambling after him at a great pace, and gaining at every jump, and his heart froze with terror. The balsams and spruces were all too low for safety. A little way before him he saw a small birch. If he could only make that he might escape. Summoning all his strength he rushed for the tree, the bear closing fast upon him. Could he spring up out of reach of the bear's awful claws?

Two yards from the tree he heard an angry snap and snarl at his heels. With a cry, he dropped his gun, and springing for the lowest bough, drew up his legs quickly after him with the horrible feeling of having them ripped asunder. To his amazement he found that the bear was not scrambling up the tree after him, but was still some paces off, with Fido skirmishing at long range. It was Fido's timely nip that had brought him to a sudden halt, and allowed Hughie to make his climb in safety.

"Good dog, Fido. Sic him! Sic him, old fellow!" cried out Hughie, but Fido was new to this kind of warfare, and at every jump of the raging brute he fled into the brush with his tail between his legs, returning, however, to the attack as the bear retired.

After driving Fido off, the bear rushed at the tree, and in a fury began tearing up its roots. Then, as if realizing the futility of this, he flung himself upon its trunk and began shaking it with great violence from side to side.

Hughie soon saw that the tree would not long stand such an attack. He slipped down to the lowest bough so that his weight might be taken from the swaying top, and encouraging Fido, awaited results.

He found himself singularly cool. Having escaped immediate danger, the hunter's instinct awoke within him, and he longed to get that bear. If he only had his gun, he would soon settle him, but the bear, unfortunately, had possession of that. He began hurriedly to cut off as stout a branch as he could to make himself a club. He was not a moment too soon, for the bear, realizing that he could neither tear up the tree by the roots nor shake his enemy out of it, decided, apparently, to go up for him.

He first set himself to get rid of Fido, which he partially succeeded in doing by chasing him a long distance off. Then, with a great rush, he flew at the tree, and with amazing rapidity began to climb.

Hughie, surprised by this swift attack, hastened to climb to the higher branches, but in a moment he saw that this would be fatal. Remembering that the bear is like the dog in his sensitive parts, he descended to meet his advancing foe, and reaching down, hit him a sharp blow on the snout. With a roar of rage and surprise the bear let go his hold, slipped to the ground, and began to tear up the earth, sneezing violently.

"Oh, if I only had that gun," groaned Hughie, "I'd get him. And if he gets away after Fido again, I believe I'll try it."

The bear now set himself to plan some new form of attack. He had been wounded, but only enough to enrage him, and his fury served to fix more firmly in his head the single purpose of getting into his grip this enemy of his in the tree, whom he appeared to have so nearly at his mercy.

Whatever his new plan might be, a necessary preliminary was getting rid of Fido, and this he proceeded to do. Round about the trees he pursued him, getting farther and farther away from the birch, till Hughie, watching his chance, slipped down the tree and ran for his gun. But no sooner had he stooped for it than the bear saw the move, and with an angry roar rushed for him.

Once more Hughie sprang for his branch, but the gun caught in the boughs and he slipped to the ground, the bear within striking distance. With a cry he sprang again, reached his bough and drew himself up, holding his precious gun safe, wondering how he had escaped. Again it was Fido that had saved him, for as the bear had gathered himself to spring, Fido, seeing his chance, rushed boldly in, and flinging himself upon the hind leg of the enraged brute, held fast. It was the boy's salvation, but alas! it was Fido's destruction, for wheeling suddenly, the bear struck a swift downward blow with his powerful front paw, and tore the whole side of the faithful brute wide open. With a howl, poor Fido dragged himself away out of reach and lay down, moaning pitifully.

The bear, realizing that he had got rid of one foe, now proceeded more cautiously to deal with the other, and began warily climbing the tree, keeping his wicked little eyes fixed upon Hughie.

Meantime, Hughie was loading his gun with all speed. He emptied his powder-horn into the muzzle, and with the bear coming slowly nearer, began to search for his bullets. Through one pocket after another his trembling fingers flew, while with the butt of his gun he menaced his approaching enemy.

"Where are those bullets?" he groaned. "Ah, here they are!" diving into his trousers pocket. "Fool of a place to keep them, too!"

He took a handful of slugs and bullets, poured them into his gun, rammed down a wadding of leaves upon all, retreating as he did so to the higher limbs, the bear following him steadily. But just as he had his cap securely fixed upon the nipple, the bear suddenly revealed his plan. Holding by his front paws, he threw his hind legs off from the trunk. It was his usual method of felling trees. The tree swayed and bent till the top almost touched the ground. But Hughie, with his legs wreathed round the trunk, brought his gun to his shoulder, and with its muzzle almost touching the breast of the hanging brute, pulled the trigger.

There was a terrific report, the bear dropped in a heap from the tree, and Hughie was hurled violently to the ground some distance away, partially stunned. He raised himself to see the bear struggle up to a sitting position, and gnashing his teeth, and flinging blood and foam from his mouth, begin to drag himself toward him. He was conscious of a languid indifference, and found himself wondering how long the bear would take to cover the distance.

But while he was thus cogitating there was a sharp, quick bark, and a great black form hurled itself at the bear's throat and bore the fierce brute to the ground.

Drawing a long sigh, Hughie sank back to the ground, with the sound of a far-away shot in his ears, and darkness veiling his eyes.

He was awakened by Don's voice anxiously calling him.

"Are you hurt much, Hughie? Did he squeeze you?"

Hughie sat up, blinking stupidly.

"What?" he asked. "Who?"

"Why, the bear, of course."

"The bear? No. Man! It's too bad you weren't here, Don," he went on, rousing himself. "He can't be gone far."

"Not very," said Don, laughing loud. "Yonder he lies."

Hughie turned his head and gazed, wondering, at the great black mass over which Don's black dogs were standing guard, and sniffing with supreme satisfaction.

Then all came back to him.

"Where's Fido?" he asked, rising. "Yes, it was Fido saved me, for sure. He tackled the bear every time he rushed at me, and hung onto him just as I climbed the tree the second time."

As he spoke he walked over to the place where he had last seen the dog. A little farther on, behind a spruce-tree, they found poor Fido, horribly mangled and dead.

Hughie stooped down over him. "Poor old boy, poor old Fido," he said, in a low voice, stroking his head.

Don turned away and walked whistling toward the bear. As he sat beside the black carcass his two dogs came to him. He threw his arms round them, saying, "Poor old Blackie! Poor Nigger!" and he understood how Hughie was feeling behind the spruce-tree beside the faithful dog that had given him his life.

As he sat there waiting for Hughie, he heard voices.

"Horo!" he shouted.

"Where are you? Is that you, Don?" It was his father's voice.

"Yes, here we are."

"Is Hughie there?" inquired another voice.

"Losh me! that's the minister," said Don. "Yes, all right," he cried aloud, as up came Long John Cameron and the minister, with Fusie and a stranger bringing up the rear.

"Fine work, this. You're fine fellows, indeed," cried Long John, "frightening people in this way."

"Where is Hughie?" said the minister, sternly.

Hughie came from behind the brush, hurriedly wiping his eyes. "Here, father," he said.

"And what are you doing here at this hour of the night, pray?" said the minister, angrily, turning toward him.

"I couldn't get home very well," replied Hughie.

"And why not, pray? Don't begin any excuses with me, sir." Nothing annoyed the minister as an attempt to excuse ill-doing.

"I guess he would have been glad enough to have got home half an hour ago, sir," broke in Don, laughing. "Look there." He pointed to the bear lying dead, with Nigger standing over him.

"The Lord save us!" said Long John Cameron, himself the greatest among the hunters of the county. "What do you say? And how did you get him? Jee-ru-piter! he's a grand one."

The old man, the minister, and Don walked about the bear in admiring procession.

"Yon's a terrible gash," said Long John, pointing to a gaping wound in the breast. "Was that your Snider, Don?"

"Not a bit of it, father. The bear's Hughie's. He killed him himself."

"Losh me! And you don't tell me! And how did you manage that, Hughie?"

"He chased me up that tree, and I guess would have got me only for Fido."

The minister gasped.

"Got you? Was he as near as that?"

"He wasn't three feet away," said Hughie, and with that he proceeded to give, in his most graphic style, a description of his great fight with the bear.

"When I heard the first shot," said Don, "I was away across the swamp. I tell you I tore back here, and when I came, what did I see but Hughie and Mr. Bear both sitting down and looking coolly at each other a few yards apart. And then Nigger downed him and I put a bullet into his heart." Don was greatly delighted, and extremely proud of Hughie's achievement.

"And how did you know about it?" asked Don of his father.

"It was the minister here came after me."

"Yes," said the minister, "it was Fusie told me you had gone off on a bear hunt, and so I went along to the Cameron's with Mr. Craven here, to see if you had got home."

Meantime, Mr. Craven had been looking Hughie over.

"Mighty plucky thing," he said. "Great nerve," and he lapsed into silence, while Fusie could not contain himself, but danced from one foot to the other with excited exclamations.

The minister had come out intending, as he said, "to teach that boy a lesson that he would remember," but as he listened to Hughie's story, his anger gave place to a great thankfulness.

"It was a great mercy, my boy," he said at length, when he was quite sure of his voice, "that you had Fido with you."

"Yes, indeed, father," said Hughie. "It was Fido saved me."

"It was the Lord's goodness," said the minister, solemnly.

"And a great mercy," said Long John, "that your lad kept his head and showed such courage. You have reason to be proud of him."

The minister said nothing just then, but at home, when recounting the exploit to the mother, he could hardly contain his pride in his son.

"Never thought the boy would have a nerve like that, he's so excitable. I had rather he killed that bear than win a medal at the university."

The mother sat silent through all the story, her cheek growing more and more pale, but not a word did she say until the tale was done, and then she said, "'Who delivereth thee from destruction.'"

"A little like David, mother, wasn't it?" said Hughie; but though there was a smile on his face, his manner and tone were earnest enough.

"Yes," said his mother, "a good deal like David, for it was the same God that delivered you both."

"Rather hard to cut Fido out of his share of the glory," said Mr. Craven, "not to speak of a cool head and a steady nerve."

Mrs. Murray regarded him for a moment or two in silence, as if meditating an answer, but finally she only said, "We shall cut no one out of the glory due to him."

At the supper-table the whole affair was discussed in all its bearings. In this discussion Hughie took little part, making light of his exploit, and giving most of the credit to Fido, and the mother wondered at the unusual reserve and gravity that had fallen upon her boy. Indeed, Hughie was wondering at himself. He had a strange new feeling in his heart. He had done a man's deed, and for the first time in his life he felt it unnecessary to glory in his deeds. He had come to a new experience, that great deeds need no voice to proclaim them. During the thrilling moments of that terrible hour he had entered the borderland of manhood, and the awe of that new world was now upon his spirit.

It was chiefly this new experience of his that was sobering him, but it helped him not a little to check his wonted boyish exuberance that at the table opposite him sat a strange young man, across whose dark, magnetic face there flitted, now and then, a lazy, cynical smile. Hughie feared that lazy smile, and he felt that it would shrivel into self-contempt any feeling of boastfulness.

The mother and Hughie said little to each other, waiting to be alone, and after Hughie had gone to his room his mother talked long with him, but when Mr. Craven, on his way to bed, heard the low, quiet tones of the mother's voice through the shut door, he knew it was not to Hughie she was speaking, and the smile upon his face lost a little of its cynicism.

Next day there was no smile when he stood with Hughie under the birch-tree, watching the lad hew flat one side, but gravely enough he took the paper on which Hughie had written, "Fido, Sept. 13th, 18--," saying as he did so, "I shall cut this for you. It is good to remember brave deeds."

CHAPTER XI

JOHN CRAVEN'S METHOD

Mr. John Craven could not be said to take his school-teaching seriously; and indeed, any one looking at his face would hardly expect him to take anything seriously, and certainly those who in his college days followed and courted and kept pace with Jack Craven, and knew his smile, would have expected from him anything other than seriousness. He appeared to himself to be enacting a kind of grim comedy, exile as he was in a foreign land, among people of a strange tongue.

He knew absolutely nothing of pedagogical method, and consequently he ignored all rules and precedents in the teaching and conduct of the school. His discipline was of a most fantastic kind. He had a feeling that all lessons were a bore, therefore he would assign the shortest and easiest of tasks. But having assigned the tasks, he expected perfection in recitation, and impressed his pupils with the idea that nothing less would pass. His ideas of order were of the loosest kind, and hence the noise at times was such that even the older pupils found it unbearable; but when the hour for recitation came, somehow a deathlike stillness fell upon the school, and the unready shivered with dread apprehension. And yet he never thrashed the boys; but his fear lay upon them, for his eyes held the delinquent with such an intensity of magnetic, penetrating power that the unhappy wretch felt as if any kind of calamity might befall him.

When one looked at John Craven's face, it was the eyes that caught and held the attention. They were black, without either gleam or glitter, indeed almost dull-- a lady once called them "smoky eyes." They looked, under lazy, half-drooping lids, like things asleep, except in moments of passion, when there appeared, far down, a glowing fire, red and terrible. At such moments it seemed as if, looking through these, one were catching sight of a soul ablaze. They were like the dull glow of a furnace through an inky night.

He was constitutionally and habitually lazy, but in a reading lesson he would rouse himself at times, and by his utterance of a single line make the whole school sit erect. Friday afternoon he gave up to what he called "the cultivation of the finer arts." On that afternoon he would bring his violin and teach the children singing, hear them read and recite, and read for them himself; and no greater punishment could be imposed upon the school than the loss of this afternoon.

"Man alive! Thomas, he's mighty queer," Hughie explained to his friend. "When he sits there with his feet on the stove smoking away and reading something or other, and letting them all gabble like a lot of ducks, it just makes me mad. But when he wakes up he puts the fear of death on you, and when he reads he makes you shiver through and through. You know that long rigmarole, 'Friends, Romans, countrymen'? I used to hate it. Well, sir, he told us about it last Friday. You know, on Friday afternoons we don't do any work, but just have songs and reading, and that sort of thing. Well, sir, last Friday he told us about the big row in Rome, and how Caesar was murdered, and then he read that thing to us. By gimmini whack! it made me hot and cold. I could hardly keep from yelling, and every one was white. And then he read that other thing, you know, about Little Nell. Used to make me sick, but, my goodness alive! do you know, before he got through the girls were wiping their eyes, and I was almost as bad, and you could have heard a pin drop. He's mighty queer, though, lazy as the mischief, and always smiling and smiling, and yet you don't feel like smiling back."

"Do you like him?" asked Thomas, bluntly.

"Dunno. I'd like to, but he won't let you, somehow. Just smiles at you, and you feel kind of small."

The reports about the master were conflicting and disquieting, and although Hughie was himself doubtful, he stood up vehemently for him at home.

"But, Hughie," protested the minister, discussing these reports, "I am told that he actually smokes in school."

Hughie was silent.

"Answer me! Does he smoke in school hours?"

"Well," confessed Hughie, reluctantly, "he does sometimes, but only after he gives us all our work to do."

"Smoke in school hours!" ejaculated Mrs. Murray, horrified.

"Well, what's the harm in that? Father smokes."

"But he doesn't smoke when he is preaching," said the mother.

"No, but he smokes right afterwards."

"But not in church."

"Well, perhaps not in church, but school's different. And anyway, he makes them read better, and write better too," said Hughie, stoutly.

"Certainly," said his father, "he is a most remarkable man. A most unusual man."

"What about your sums, Hughie?" asked his mother.

"Don't know. He doesn't bother much with that sort of thing, and I'm just as glad."

"You ought really to speak to him about it," said Mrs. Murray, after Hughie had left the room.

"Well, my dear," said the minister, smiling, "you heard what Hughie said. It would be rather awkward for me to speak to him about smoking. I think, perhaps, you had better do it."

"I am afraid," said his wife, with a slight laugh, "it would be just as awkward for me. I wonder what those Friday afternoons of his mean," she continued.

"I am sure I don't know, but everywhere throughout the section I hear the children speak of them. We'll just drop in and see. I ought to visit the school, you know, very soon."

And so they did. The master was surprised, and for a moment appeared uncertain what to do. He offered to put the classes through their regular lessons, but at once there was a noisy outcry against this on the part of the school, which, however, was effectually and immediately quelled by the quiet suggestion on the master's part that anything but perfect order would be fatal to the programme. And upon the minister requesting that the usual exercises proceed, the master smilingly agreed.

"We make Friday afternoons," he said, "at once a kind of reward day for good work during the week, and an opportunity for the cultivation of some of the finer arts."

And certainly he was a master in this business. He had strong dramatic instincts, and a remarkable power to stimulate and draw forth the emotions.

When the programme of singing, recitations, and violin-playing was finished, there were insistent calls on every side for "Mark Antony." It appeared to be the 'piece de resistance' in the minds of the children.

"What does this mean?" inquired the minister, as the master stood smiling at his pupils.

"Oh, they are demanding a little high tragedy," he said, "which I sometimes give them. It assists in their reading lessons," he explained, apologetically, and with that he gave them what Hughie called, "that rigmarole beginning, 'Friends, Romans, countrymen,'" Mark Antony's immortal oration.

"Well," said the minister, as they drove away from the school, "what do you think of that, now?"

"Marvelous!" exclaimed his wife. "What dramatic power, what insight, what interpretation!"

"You may say so," exclaimed her husband. "What an actor he would make!"

"Yes," said his wife, "or what a minister he would make! I understand, now, his wonderful influence over Hughie, and I am afraid."

"O, he can't do Hughie any harm with things like that," replied her husband, emphatically.

"No, but Hughie now and then repeats some of his sayings about-- about religion and religious convictions, that I don't like. And then he is hanging about that Twentieth store altogether too much, and I fancied I noticed something strange about him last Friday evening when he came home so late."

"O, nonsense," said the minister. "His reputation has prejudiced you, and that is not fair, and your imagination does the rest."

"Well, it is a great pity that he should not do something with himself," replied his wife. "There are great possibilities in that young man."

"He does not take himself seriously enough," said her husband. "That is the chief trouble with him."

And this was apparently Jack Craven's opinion of himself, as is evident from his letter to his college friend, Ned Maitland.

"Dear Ned:--

"For the last two months I have been seeking to adjust myself to my surroundings, and find it no easy business. I have struck the land of the Anakim, for the inhabitants are all of 'tremenjous' size, and indeed, 'tremenjous' in all their ways, more particularly in their religion. Religion is all over the place. You are liable to come upon a boy anywhere perched on a fence corner with a New Testament in his hand, and on Sunday the 'tremenjousness' of their religion is overwhelming. Every other interest in life, as meat, drink, and dress, are purely incidental to the main business of the day, which is the delivering, hearing, and discussing of sermons.

"The padre, at whose house I am very happily quartered, is a 'tremenjous' preacher. He has visions, and gives them to me. He gives me chills and thrills as well, and has discovered to me a conscience, a portion of my anatomy that I had no suspicion of possessing.

"The congregation is like the preacher. They will sit for two hours, and after a break of a few minutes they will sit again for two hours, listening to sermons; and even the interval is somewhat evenly divided between their bread and cheese in the churchyard and the discussion of the sermon they have just listened to. They are great on theology. One worthy old party tackled me on my views of the sermon we had just heard; after a little preliminary sparring I went to my corner. I often wonder in what continent I am.

"The school, a primitive little log affair, has much run to seed, but offers opportunity for repose. I shall avoid any unnecessary excitement in this connection.

"In private life the padre is really very decent. We have great smokes together, and talks. On all subjects he has very decided opinions, and in everything but religion, liberal views. I lure him into philosophic discussions, and overwhelm him with my newest and biggest metaphysical terms, which always reduce his enormous cocksureness to more reasonable dimensions.

"The minister's wife is quite another proposition. She argues, too, but unfortunately she asks questions, in the meekest way possible acknowledging her ignorance of my big terms, and insisting upon definitions and exact meanings, and then it's all over with me. How she ever came to this far land, heaven knows, and none but heaven can explain such waste. Having no kindred soul to talk with, I fancy she enjoys conversation with myself, (sic) revels in music, is transported to the fifth heaven by my performance on the violin, but evidently pities me and regards me as dangerous. But, my dear Maitland, after a somewhat wide and varied experience of fine ladies, I give you my verdict that here among the Anakim, and in this wild, woody land, is a lady fine and fair and saintly. She will bother me, I know. Her son Hughie (he of the bear), of whom I told you, the lad with the face of an angel and the temper of an angel, but of a different color--her son Hughie she must make into a scholar. And no wonder, for already he has attained a remarkable degree of excellence, by the grace, not of the little log school, however, I venture to shy. His mother has been at him. But now she feels that something more is needed, and for that she turns to me. You will be able to see the humor of it, but not the pathos. She wants to make a man out of her boy, 'a noble, pure-hearted gentleman,' and this she lays upon me! Did I hear you laugh? Smile not, it is the most tragic of pathos. Upon me, Jack Craven, the despair of the professors, the terror of the watch, the--alas! you know only too well. My tongue clave to the roof of my mouth, and before I could cry, 'Heaven forbid that I should have a hand in the making of your boy!' she accepted my pledge to do her desire for her young angel with the OTHER-angelic temper.

"And now, my dear Ned, is it for my sins that I am thus pursued? What is awaiting me I know not. What I shall do with the young cub I have not the ghostliest shadow of an idea. Shall I begin by thrashing him soundly? I have refrained so far; I hate the role of executioner. Or shall I teach him boxing? The gloves are a great educator, and are at times what the padre would call 'means of grace.'

"But what will become of me? Shall I become prematurely aged, or shall I become a saint? Expect anything from your most devoted, but most sorely bored and perplexed,

"J. C."

CHAPTER XII

THE DOWNFALL

In one point the master was a great disappointment to Hughie; he could not be persuaded to play shinny. The usual challenge had come up from the Front, with its more than usual insolence, and Hughie, who now ranked himself among the big boys, felt the shame and humiliation to be intolerable. By the most strenuous exertions he started the game going with the first fall of snow, but it was difficult to work up any enthusiasm for the game in the face of Foxy's very determined and weighty opposition, backed by the master's lazy indifference. For, in spite of Hughie's contempt and open sneers, Foxy had determined to reopen his store with new and glowing attractions. He seemed to have a larger command of capital than ever, and he added several very important departments to his financial undertaking.

The rivalry between Hughie and Foxy had become acute, but besides this, there was in Hughie's heart a pent-up fierceness and longing for revenge that he could with difficulty control. And though he felt pretty certain that in an encounter with Foxy he would come off second best, and though in consequence he delayed that encounter as long as possible, he never let Foxy suspect his fear of him, and waited with some anxiety for the inevitable crisis.

Upon one thing Hughie was resolved, that the challenge from the Front should be accepted, and that they should no longer bear the taunt of cowardice, but should make a try, even though it meant certain defeat.

His first step had been the organization of the shinny club. His next step was to awaken the interest of the master. But in vain he enlarged upon the boastfulness and insolence of the Front; in vain he recounted the achievements of their heroes of old, who in those brave days had won victory and fame over all comers for their school and county; the master would not be roused to anything more than a languid interest in the game. And this was hardly to be wondered at, for shinny in the snow upon the roadway in front of the school was none too exciting. But from the day when the game was transferred to the mill-pond, one Saturday afternoon when the North and South met in battle, the master's indifference vanished, for it turned out that he was an enthusiastic skater, and as Hughie said, "a whirlwind on the ice."

After that day shinny was played only upon the ice, and the master, assuming the position of coach, instituted a more scientific style of game, and worked out a system of combined play that made even small boys dangerous opponents to boys twice their size and weight. Under his guidance it was that the challenge to the Front was so worded as to make the contest a game on ice, and to limit the number of the team to eleven. Formerly the number had been somewhat indefinite, varying from fifteen to twenty, and the style of play a general melee. Hughie was made captain of the shinny team, and set himself, under the master's direction, to perfect their combination and team play.

The master's unexpected interest in the shinny game was the first and chief cause of Foxy's downfall as leader of the school, and if Hughie had possessed his soul in patience he might have enjoyed the spectacle of Foxy's overthrow without involving himself in the painful consequences which his thirst for vengeance and his vehement desire to accomplish Foxy's ruin brought upon him.

The story of the culmination of the rivalry between Hughie and Foxy is preserved in John Craven's second letter to his friend Edward Maitland. The letter also gives an account of the master's own undoing--an undoing which bore fruit to the end of his life.

"Dear Ned:--

"I hasten to correct the false impression my previous letter must have conveyed to you. It occurs to me that I suggested that this school afforded unrivaled opportunities for repose. Further acquaintance reveals to me the fact that it is the seething center of the most nerve-racking excitement. The life of the school is reflected in the life of the community, and the throbs of excitement that vibrate from the school are felt in every home of the section. We are in the thick of preparations for a deadly contest with the insolent, benighted, boastful, but hitherto triumphant Front, in the matter of shinny. You know my antipathy to violent sports, and you will find some difficulty in picturing me an enthusiastic trainer and general director of the Twentieth team, flying about, wildly gesticulating with a club, and shrieking orders, imprecations, cautions, encouragements, in the most frantic manner, at as furious a company of little devils as ever went joyously to battle.

"Then, as if this were not excitement enough, I am made the unwitting spectator of a truly Homeric contest, bloodier by far than many of those fought on the plains of windy Troy, between the rival leaders of the school, to wit, Hughie of the angelic face and OTHER-angelic temper, and an older and much heavier boy, who rejoices in the cognomen of 'Foxy,' as being accurately descriptive at once of the brilliance of his foliage and of his financial tactics.

"It appears that for many months this rivalry has existed, but I am convinced that there is more in the struggle than appears on the surface. There is some dark and deadly mystery behind it all that only adds, of course, to the thrilling interest it holds for me.

"Long before I arrived on the arena, which was an open space in the woods in front of what Foxy calls his store, wild shrieks and yells fell upon my ears, as if the aboriginal denizens of the forest had returned. Quietly approaching, I soon guessed the nature of the excitement, and being unwilling to interfere until I had thoroughly grasped the ethical and other import of the situation, I shinned up a tree, and from this point of vantage took in the spectacle. It appeared from Foxy's violent accusations that Hughie had been guilty of wrecking the store, which, by the way, the latter utterly despises and contemns. The following interesting and striking conversation took place:

"'What are you doing in my store, anyway?' says he of the brilliant foliage. 'You're just a thief, that's what you are, and a sneaking thief.'

"Promptly the lie comes back. 'I wasn't touching your rotten stuff!' and again the lie is exchanged.

"Immediately there is demand from the spectators that the matter be argued to a demonstration, and thereupon one of the larger boys, wishing to precipitate matters and to furnish a casus belli, puts a chip upon Hughie's shoulder and dares Foxy to knock it off. But Hughie flings the chip aside.

"'Go away with yourself and your chip. I'm not going to fight for any chip.'

"Yells of derision, 'Cowardy, cowardy, custard,' 'Give him a good cuffing, Foxy,' 'He's afraid,' and so forth. And indeed, Hughie appears none too anxious to prove his innocence and integrity upon the big and solid body of his antagonist.

"Foxy, much encouraged by the clamor of his friends, deploys in force in front of his foe, shouting, 'Come on, you little thief!'

"'I'm not a thief! I didn't touch one of your things!'

"'Whether you touched my things or not, you're a thief, anyway, and you know you are. You stole money, and I know it, and you know it yourself.'

"To this Hughie strangely enough makes no reply, wherein lies the mystery. But though he makes no reply he faces up boldly to Foxy and offers battle. This is evidently a surprise to Foxy, who contents himself with threats as to what he can do with his one hand tied behind his back, and what he will do in a minute, while Hughie waits, wasting no strength upon words.

"Finally Foxy strides to his store door, and apparently urged to frenzy by the sight of the wreckage therein, comes back and lands a sharp cuff on his antagonist's ear.

"It is all that is needed. As if he had touched a spring, Hughie flew at him wildly, inconsequently making a windmill of his arms. But fortunately he runs foul of one of Foxy's big fists, and falls back with spouting nose. Enthusiastic yells from Foxy's following. And Foxy, having done much better than he expected, is encouraged to pursue his advantage.

"Meantime the blood is being mopped off Hughie's face with a snowball, his tears flowing equally with his blood.

"'Wait till to-morrow,' urges Fusie, his little French fidus Achates.

"'To-morrow!' yells Hughie, suddenly. 'No, but now! I'll kill the lying, sneaking, white-faced beast now, or I'll die myself!' after which heroic resolve he flings himself, blood and tears, upon the waiting Foxy, and this time with better result, for Foxy, waiting the attack with arms up and eyes shut, finds himself pummeled all over the face, and after a few moments of ineffectual resistance, turns, and in quite the Homeric way seeks safety in flight, followed by the furious and vengeful Achilles, and the jeering shouts of the bloodthirsty but disappointed rabble.

"As I have said, the mystery behind it remains unsolved, but Foxy's reign is at an end, and with him goes the store, for which I am devoutly thankful.

"I would my tale ended here with the downfall of Foxy, but, my dear Ned, I have to record a sadder and more humiliating downfall than that--the abject and utter collapse of my noble self. I have once more played the fool, and played into the hands of the devil, mine own familiar and well-beloved devil.

"The occasion I need not enlarge upon; it always waits. A long day's skate, a late supper with some of the wilder and more reckless outcasts of this steady-going community that frequent the back store, results in my appearing at the manse door late at night, very unsteady of leg and incoherent of speech. By a most unhappy chance, a most scurvy trick my familiar devil played upon me, the door is opened by the minister's wife. I can see her look of fear, horror, and loathing yet. It did more to pull me together than a cold bath, so that I saved myself the humiliation of speech and escaped to my room.

"And now, what do you think? Reproaches, objurgations, and final dismissal on the part of the padre, tearful exhortations to repentance on the part of his wife? Not a bit. If you believe me, sir, my unhappy misadventure remains a secret with her. She told not a soul. Remarkably fine, I call that. And what more, think you? A cold and haughty reserve, or a lofty pity, with the fearful expectation of judgment? Not in the least. Only a little added kindness, a deeper note to the frank, sympathetic interest she has always shown, and that is all. My dear chap, I offered to leave, but when she looked at me with those great hazel-brown eyes of hers and said, 'Why should you go? Would it be better for you any place else?' I found myself enjoying the luxury of an entirely new set of emotions, which I shall not analyze to you. But I feel more confident than ever that I shall either die early or end in being a saint.

"And now, do you know, she persists in ignoring that anything has taken place, talks to me about her young men and her hopes for them, the work she would do for them, and actually asks my assistance! It appears that ever since their Great Revival, which is the beginning of days to them, events being dated from before the Great Revival or after, some of these young men have a desire to be ministers, or think they have. It is really her desire, I suspect, for them. The difficulty is, preparation for college. In this she asks my help. The enormous incongruity of the situation does not appear to strike her, that I, the--too many unutterable things--should be asked to prepare these young giants, with their 'tremenjous' religious convictions, for the ministry; nevertheless I yield myself to do anything and everything she lays upon me. I repeat, I shall without doubt end in being a saint myself, and should not be surprised to find myself with these 'tremenjous' young men on the way to Holy Orders. Fancy the good Doctor's face! He would suspect a lurking pleasantry in it all.

"This letter, I know, will render chaotic all your conceptions of me, and in this chaos of mind I can heartily sympathize. What the next chapter will be, God only knows! It depends upon how my familiar devil behaves himself. Meantime, I am parleying with him, and with some anxiety as to the result subscribe myself,

"Your friend,

"J. C."

CHAPTER XIII

THE FIRST ROUND

The challenge from the Front was for the best two out of three, the first game to be played the last day of the year. Steadily, under Craven's coaching, the Twentieth team were perfected in their systematic play; for although Craven knew nothing of shinny, he had captained the champion lacrosse team of the province of Quebec, and the same general rules of defense and attack could be applied with equal success to the game of shinny. The team was greatly strengthened by the accession of Thomas Finch and Don Cameron, both of whom took up the school again with a view to college. With Thomas in goal, Hughie said he felt as if a big hole had been filled up behind him.

The master caused a few preliminary skirmishes with neighboring teams to be played by way of practice, and by the time the end of the year had come, he felt confident that the team would not disgrace their school. His confidence was not ill-founded.

"We have covered ourselves with glory," he writes to his friend Ned Maitland, "for we have whipped to a finish the arrogant and mighty Front. I am more than ever convinced that I shall have to take a few days off and get away to Montreal, or some other retired spot, to recover from the excitement of the last week.

"Under my diligent coaching, in which, knowing nothing whatever of shinny, I have striven to introduce something of the lacrosse method, our team got into really decent fighting trim. Under the leadership of their captain, who has succeeded in infusing his own fierce and furious temper into his men, they played like little demons, from the drop of the ball till the game was scored. 'Furious' is the word, for they and their captain play with headlong fury, and that, I might say, is about their only defect, for if they ever should run into a bigger team, who had any semblance of head about them, and were not merely feet, they would surely come to grief.

"I cannot stay to recount our victory. Let it suffice that we were driven down in two big sleigh-loads by Thomas Finch, the back wall of our defense, and Don Cameron, who plays in the right of the forward line, both great, strapping fellows, who are to be eventually, I believe, members of my preparatory class.

"The Front came forth, cheerful, big, confident, trusting in the might of their legs. We are told that the Lord taketh no pleasure in the legs of man, and this is true in the game of shinny. Not legs alone, but heart and head win, with anything like equal chances.

"Game called, 2:30; Captain Hughie has the drop; seizes the ball, passes it to Fusie, who rushes, passes back to Hughie, who has arrived in the vicinity of the enemy's goal, and shoots, swift and straight, a goal. Time, 30 seconds.

"Again and again my little demons pierce the heavy, solid line of the Front defense, and score, the enemy, big and bewildered, being chiefly occupied in watching them do it. By six o'clock that evening I had them safe at the manse in a condition of dazed jubilation, quite unable to realize the magnificence of their achievement. They had driven twelve miles down, played a two hours' game of shinny, score eight to two, and were back safe and sound, bearing with them victory and some broken shins, equally proud of both.

"There is a big supper at the manse, prepared, I believe, with the view of consolation, but transformed into a feast of triumph, the minister being enthusiastically jubilant over the achievement of his boys, his wife, if possible, even more so. The heroes feed themselves to fullness, amazing and complete, the minister holds a thanksgiving service, in which I have no doubt my little demons most earnestly join, after which they depart to shed the radiance of their glory throughout the section.

"And now I have to recount another experience of mine, quite unique and altogether inexplicable. It appears that in this remarkable abode--I would call it 'The Saint's Rest' were it not for the presence of others than saints, and for the additional fact that there is little rest for the saint who makes her dwelling here--in this abode there prevails the quaint custom of watching the death of the old year and the birth of the new. It is made the occasion of religious and heart-searching rite. As the solemn hour of midnight draws on, a silence falls upon the family, all of whom, with the exception of the newest infant, are present. It is the family festival of the year.

"'And what will they be doing at your home, Mr. Craven?' inquires the minister. The contrast that rose before my mind was vivid enough, for having received my invitation to a big dance, I knew my sweet sisters would be having a jolly wild time about that moment. My answer, given I feel in a somewhat flippant tone, appears to shock my shinny captain of the angelic face, who casts a honor- stricken glance at his mother, and waits for the word of reproof that he thinks is due from the padre's lips.

"But before it falls the mother interposes with 'They will miss you greatly this evening.' It was rather neatly done, and I think I appreciated it.

"The rite proceeds. The initial ceremony is the repeating of a verse of Scripture all round, and to save my life nothing comes to my mind but the words,

'Remember Lot's wife.' As I cannot see the appropriateness of the quotation, I pass.

"Five minutes before the stroke of twelve, they sing the Scottish paraphrase beginning, 'O God of Bethel.' I do not suppose you ever heard it, but it is a beautiful hymn, and singularly appropriate to the hour. In this I lend assistance with my violin, the tune being the very familiar one of 'Auld Lang Syne,' associated in my mind, however, with occasions somewhat widely diverse from this. I assure you I am thankful that my part is instrumental, for the whole business is getting onto my emotions in a disturbing manner, and especially when I allow my eyes to linger for a moment or two on the face of the lady, the center of the circle, who is deliberately throwing away her fine culture and her altogether beautiful soul upon the Anakim here, and with a beautiful unconsciousness of anything like sacrifice, is now thanking God for the privilege of doing so. I have some moments of rare emotional luxury, those moments that are next to tears.

"Then the padre offers one of those heart-racking prayers of his that, whether they reach anything outside or not, somehow get down into one's vitals, and stir up remorses, and self-condemnings, and longings unutterable. Then they all kiss the mother and wish her a Happy New-Year.

"My boy, my dear boy, I have never known deeper moments than those. And when I went to shake hands with her, she seemed so like a queen receiving homage, that without seeming to feel I was making a fool of myself, I did the Queen Victoria act, and saluted her hand. It is wonderful how great moments discover the lady to you. She must have known how I was feeling, for with a very beautiful grace, she said, 'Let me be your mother for to-night,' and by Jove, she kissed me. I have been kissed before, and have kissed some women in my time, but that is the only kiss I can remember, and s'help me Bob, I'll never kiss another till I kiss my wife.

"And then and there, Maitland, I swore by all that I knew of God, and by everything sacred in life, that I'd quit the past and be worthy of her trust; for the mischief of it is, she will persist in trusting you, puts you on your honor noblesse oblige business, and all that. I think I told you that I might end in being a saint. That dream I have surrendered, but, by the grace of heaven, I'm going to try to be a man. And I am going to play shinny with those boys, and if I can help them to win that match, and the big game of life, I will do it.

"As witness my hand and seal, this first day of January, 18--

"J. C."

CHAPTER XIV

THE FINAL ROUND

After the New-Year the school filled up with big boys, some of whom had returned with the idea of joining the preparatory class for college, which the minister had persuaded John Craven to organize.

Shinny, however, became the absorbing interest for all the boys, both big and little. This interest was intensified by the rumors that came up from the Front, for it was noised through the Twentieth section that Dan Munro, whose father was a cousin of Archie Munro, the former teacher, had come from Marrintown and taken charge of the Front school, and that, being used to the ice game, and being full of tricks and swift as a bird, he was an exceedingly dangerous man. More than that, he was training his team with his own tricks, and had got back to school some of the old players, among whom were no less renowned personages than Hec Ross and Jimmie "Ben." Jimmie Ben, to wit, James son of Benjamin McEwen, was more famed for his prowess as a fighter than for his knowledge of the game of shinny, but every one who saw him play said he was "a terror." Further, it was rumored that there was a chance of them getting for goal Farquhar McRae, "Little Farquhar," or "Farquhar Bheg" (pronounced "vaick"), as he was euphoniously called, who presumably had once been little, but could no longer claim to be so, seeing that he was six feet, and weighed two hundred pounds.

It behooved the Twentieth team, therefore, to bestir themselves with all diligence, and in this matter Hughie gave no rest either to himself or to any one else likely to be of use in perfecting his team. For Hughie had been unanimously chosen captain, in spite of his protests that the master or one of the big boys should hold that place. But none of the big boys knew the new game as perfectly as Hughie, and the master had absolutely refused, saying, "You beat them once, Hughie, and you can do it again." And as the days and weeks went on, Hughie fully justified the team's choice of him as captain. He developed a genius for organization, a sureness of judgment, and a tact in management, as well as a skill and speed in play, that won the confidence of every member of his team. He set himself resolutely to banish any remaining relics of the ancient style of play. In the old game every one rushed to hit the ball without regard to direction or distance, and the consequence was, that from end to end of the field a mob of yelling, stick- waving players more or less aimlessly followed in the wake of the ball. But Hughie and the master changed all that, forced the men to play in their positions, training them never to drive wildly forward, but to pass to a man, and to keep their clubs down and their mouths shut.

The striking characteristic of Hughie's own playing was a certain fierceness, amounting almost to fury, so that when he was in the attack he played for every ounce there was in him. His chief weakness lay in his tempestuous temper, which he found difficult to command, but as he worked his men from day to day, and week to week, the responsibility of his position and the magnitude of the issues at stake helped him to a self-control quite remarkable in him.

As the fateful day drew near the whole section was stirred with an intense interest and excitement, in which even the grave and solemn elders shared, and to a greater degree, the minister and his wife.

At length the day, as all days great and small, actually arrived. A big crowd awaited the appearance of "the folks from the Front." They were expected about two, but it was not till half-past that there was heard in the distance the sound of the bagpipes.

"Here they are! That's Alan the cooper's pipes," was the cry, and before long, sure enough there appeared Alphonse le Roque driving his French-Canadian team, the joy and pride of his heart, for Alphonse was a born horse-trainer, and had taught his French- Canadians many extraordinary tricks. On the dead gallop he approached the crowd till within a few yards, when, at a sudden command, they threw themselves upon their haunches, and came almost to a standstill. With a crack of his long whip Alphonse gave the command, "Deesplay yousef!" At once his stout little team began to toss their beautiful heads, and broke into a series of prancing curves that would not have shamed a pair of greyhounds. Then, as they drew up to the stopping-point, he gathered up his lines, and with another crack of his whip, cried, "Salute ze ladies!" when, with true equine courtesy, they rose upon their hind legs and gracefully pawed the empty air. Finally, after depositing his load amid the admiring exclamations of the crowd, he touched their tails with the point of his whip, gave a sudden "Whish!" and like hounds from the leash his horses sprang off at full gallop.

One after another the teams from the Front swung round and emptied their loads.

"Man! what a crowd!" said Hughie to Don. "There must be a hundred at least."

"Yes, and there's Hec Ross and Jimmie Ben," said Don, "and sure enough, Farquhar Begh. We'll be catching it to-day, whatever," continued Don, cheerfully.

"Pshaw! we licked as big men before. It isn't size," said Hughie, with far more confidence than he felt.

It was half an hour before the players were ready to begin. The rules of the game were few and simple. The play was to be one hour each way, with a quarter of an hour rest between. There was to be no tripping, no hitting on the shins when the ball was out of the scrimmage, and all disputes were to be settled by the umpire, who on this occasion was the master of the Sixteenth school.

"He's no good," grumbled Hughie to his mother, who was even more excited than her boy himself. "He can't play himself, and he's too easy scared."

"Never mind," said his mother, brightly; "perhaps he won't have much to do."

"Much to do! Well, there's Jimmie Ben, and he's an awful fighter, but I'm not going to let him frighten me," said Hughie, savagely; "and there's Dan Munro, too, they say he's a terror, and Hec Ross. Of course we've got just as good men, but they won't fight. Why, Johnnie 'Big Duncan' and Don, there, are as good as any of them, but they won't fight."

The mother smiled a little.

"What a pity! But why should they fight? Fighting is not shinny."

"No, that's what the master says. And he's right enough, too, but it's awful hard when a fellow doesn't play fair, when he trips you up or clubs you on the shins when you're not near the ball. You feel like hitting him back."

"Yes, but that's the very time to show self-control."

"I know. And that's what the master says."

"Of course it is," went on his mother. "That's what the game is for, to teach the boys to command their tempers. You remember 'he that ruleth his spirit is better than he that taketh a city.'

"O, it's all right," said Hughie, "and easy enough to talk about."

"What's easy enough to talk about?" asked the master, coming up.

"Taking a city," said Mrs. Murray, smiling at him.

The master looked puzzled.

"Mother means," said Hughie, "keeping one's temper in shinny. But I'm telling her it's pretty hard when a fellow clubs you on the shins when you're away from the ball."

"Yes, of course it's hard," said the master, "but it's better than being a cad," which brought a quick flush to Hughie's face, but helped him more than anything else to keep himself in hand that day.

"Can't understand a man," said the master, "who goes into a game and then quits it to fight. If it's fighting, why fight, but if it's shinny, play the game. Big team against us, eh, captain?" he continued, looking at the Front men, who were taking a preliminary spin upon the ice, "and pretty swift, too."

"If they play fair, I don't mind," said Hughie. "I'm not afraid of them; but if they get slugging--"

"Well, if they get slugging," said the master, "we'll play the game and win, sure."

"Well, it's time to begin," said Hughie, and with a good by to his mother he turned away.

"Remember, take a city," she called out after him.

"All right, muzzie, I'll remember."

In a few moments the teams were in position opposite each other. The team from the Front made a formidable show in weight and muscle. At the right of the forward line stood the redoubtable Dan Munro, the stocky, tricky, fierce captain of the Front team, and with him three rather small boys in red shirts. The defense consisted of Hec Ross, the much-famed and much-feared Jimmie Ben, while in goal, sure enough, stood the immense and solid bulk of Farquhar Bheg. The center was held by four boys of fair size and weight.

In the Twentieth team the forward line was composed of Jack Ross, Curly Ross's brother, Fusie, Davie Scotch, and Don Cameron. The center was played by Hughie, with three little chaps who made up for their lack of weight by their speed and skill. The defense consisted of Johnnie "Big Duncan," to wit, John, the son of Big Duncan Campbell, on the left hand, and the master on the right, backed up by Thomas Finch in goal, who much against his will was in the game that day. His heart was heavy within him, for he saw, not the gleaming ice and the crowding players, but "the room" at home, and his mother, with her pale, patient face, sitting in her chair. His father, he knew, would be beside her, and Jessac would be flitting about. "But for all that, she'll have a long day," he said to himself, for only his loyalty to the school and to Hughie had brought him to the game that day.

When play was called, Hughie, with Fusie immediately behind him, stood facing Dan in the center with one of the little Red Shirts at his back. It was Dan's drop. He made a pass or two, then shot between his legs to a Red Shirt, who, upon receiving, passed far out to Red Shirt number three, who flew along the outer edge and returned swiftly to Dan, now far up the other side. Like the wind Dan sped down the line, dodged Johnnie Big Duncan easily, and shot from the corner, straight, swift, and true, a goal.

"One for the Front!" Eleven shinny-sticks went up in the air, the bagpipes struck up a wild refrain, big Hec Ross and Jimmie Ben danced a huge, unwieldy, but altogether jubilant dance round each other, and then settled down to their places, for it was Hughie's drop.

Hughie took the ball from the umpire and faced Dan with some degree of nervousness, for Dan was heavy and strong, and full of confidence. After a little manoeuvering he dropped the ball between Dan's legs, but Dan, instead of attending to the ball, charged full upon him and laid him flat, while one of the Red Shirts, seizing the ball, flew off with it, supported by a friendly Red Shirt on either side of him, with Dan following hard.

Right through the crowd dodged the Red Shirts till they came up to the Twentieth line of defense, when forth came Johnnie Big Duncan in swift attack. But the little Red Shirt who had the ball, touching it slightly to the right, tangled himself up in Johnnie Big Duncan's legs and sent him sprawling, while Dan swiped the ball to another Red Shirt who had slipped in behind the master, for there was no such foolishness as off-side in that game. Like lightning the Red Shirt caught the ball, and rushing at Thomas, shot furiously at close quarters. Goal number two for the Front!

Again on all sides rose frantic cheers. "The Front! The Front! Murro forever!" Two games had been won, and not a Twentieth man had touched the ball. With furtive, uncertain glances the men of the Twentieth team looked one at the other, and all at their captain, as if seeking explanation of this extraordinary situation.

"Well," said Hughie, in a loud voice, to the master, and with a careless laugh, though at his heart he was desperate, "they are giving us a little taste of our own medicine."

The master dropped to buckle his skate, deliberately unwinding the strap, while the umpire allowed time.

"Give me a hand with this, Hughie," he called, and Hughie skated up to him.

"Well," said Craven, smiling up into Hughie's face, "that's a good, swift opening, isn't it?"

"Oh, it's terrible," groaned Hughie. "They're going to lick us off the ice."

"Well," replied the master, slowly, "I wouldn't be in a hurry to say so. We have a hundred minutes and more to win in yet. Now, don't you see that their captain is their great card. Suppose you let the ball go for a game or two, and stick to Dan. Trail him, never let him shake you. The rest of us will take care of the game."

"All right," said Hughie, "I'll stick to him," and off he set for the center.

As the loser, Hughie again held the drop. He faced Dan with determination to get that ball out to Fusie, and somehow he felt in his bones that he should succeed in doing this. Without any preliminary he dropped, and knocked the ball toward Fusie.

But this was evidently what Dan expected, for as soon as Hughie made the motion to drop he charged hard upon the waiting Fusie. Hughie, however, had his plan as well, for immediately upon the ball leaving his stick, he threw himself in Dan's way, checking him effectually, and allowing Fusie, with Don and Scotchie following, to get away.

The Front defense, however, was too strong, and the ball came shooting back toward the line of Reds, one of whom, making a short run, passed far out to Dan on the right. But before the latter could get up speed, Hughie was upon him, and ignoring the ball, blocked and bothered and checked him, till one of the Twentieth centers, rushing in, secured it for his side.

"Ha! well done, captain!" came Craven's voice across the ice, and Hughie felt his nerve come back. If he could hold Dan, that deadly Front combination might be broken.

Meantime Don had secured the ball from Craven, and was rushing up his right wing.

"Here you are, Hughie," he cried, shooting across the Front goal.

Hughie sprang to receive, but before he could shoot Dan was upon him, checking so hard that Hughie was sent sprawling to the ice, while Dan shot away with the ball.

But before he had gone very far Hughie was after him like a whirlwind, making straight for his own goal, so that by the time Dan had arrived at shooting distance, Hughie was again upon him, and while in the very act of steadying himself for his try at the goal, came crashing into him with such fierceness of attack that Dan was flung aside, while Johnnie Big Duncan, capturing the ball, sent it across to the master.

It was the master's first chance for the day. With amazing swiftness and dexterity he threaded the outer edge of the ice, and with a sudden swerve across, avoided the throng that had gathered to oppose him, and then with a careless ease, as if it were a matter of little importance, he dodged in between the heavy Front defense, shot his goal, and skated back coolly to his place.

The Twentieth's moment had come, and both upon the ice and upon the banks the volume and fierceness of the cheering testified to the intensity of the feeling that had been so long pent up.

That game had revealed to Hughie two important facts: the first, that he was faster than Dan in a straight race; and the second, that it would be advisable to feed the master, for it was clearly apparent that there was not his equal upon the ice in dodging.

"That was well done, captain," said Craven to Hughie, as he was coolly skating back to his position.

"A splendid run, sir," cried Hughie, in return.

"Oh, the run was easy. It was your check there that did the trick. That's the game," he continued, lowering his voice. "It's hard on you, though. Can you stand it?"

"Well, I can try for a while," said Hughie, confidently.

"If you can," said the master, "we've got them," and Hughie settled down into the resolve that, cost what it might, he would stick like a leech to Dan.

He imparted his plan to Fusie, adding, "Now, whenever you see me tackle Dan, run in and get the ball. I'm not going to bother about it."

Half an hour had gone. The score stood two to one in favor of the Front, but the result every one felt to be still uncertain. That last attack of Hughie's, and the master's speedy performance, gave some concern to the men of the Front, and awakened a feeling of confidence in the Twentieth team.

But Dan, wise general that he was, saw the danger, and gave his commands ere he faced off for the new game.

"When that man Craven gets it," he said to the men of the center, "make straight for the goal. Never mind the ball."

The wisdom of this order became at once evident, for when in the face-off he secured the ball, Hughie clung so tenaciously to his heels and checked him so effectually, that he was forced to resign it to the Reds, who piercing the Twentieth center, managed to scurry up the ice with the ball between them. But when, met by Craven and Johnnie Big Duncan, they passed across to Dan, Hughie again checked so fiercely that Johnnie Big Duncan secured the ball, passed back to the master, who with another meteoric flash along the edge of the field broke through the Front's defense, and again shot.

It was only Farquhar Bheg's steady coolness that saved the goal. It was a near enough thing, however, to strike a sudden chill to the heart of the Front goal-keeper, and to make Dan realize that something must be done to check these dangerous rushes of Craven.

"Get in behind the defense there, and stay there," he said to two of his centers, and his tone indicated that his serene confidence in himself and his team was slightly shaken. Hughie's close checking was beginning to chafe him, for his team in their practice had learned to depend unduly upon him.

Noticing Dan's change in the disposition of his men, Hughie moved up two of his centers nearer to the Front defense.

"Get into their way," he said "and give the master a clear field."

But this policy only assisted Dan's plan of defense, for the presence of so many players before the Front goal filled up the ice to such an extent that Craven's rushes were impeded by mere numbers.

For some time Dan watched the result of his tactics well satisfied, remaining himself for the time in the background. During one of the pauses, when the ball was out of play, he called one of the little Reds to him.

"Look here," he said, "you watch this. Right after one of those rushes of Craven's, don't follow him down, but keep up to your position. I'll get the ball to you somehow, and then you'll have a chance to shoot. No use passing to me, for this little son of a gun is on my back like a flea on a dog." Dan was seriously annoyed.

The little Red passed the word around and patiently waited his chance. Once and again the plan failed, chiefly because Dan could not get the ball out of the scrimmage, but at length, when Hughie had been tempted to rush in with the hope of putting in a shot, the ball slid out of the scrimmage, and Dan, swooping down upon it, passed swiftly to the waiting Red who immediately shot far out to his alert wing, and then rushing down the center and slipping past Johnnie Big Duncan, who had gone forth to meet Dan coming down the right, and the master who was attending to the little Red on the wing, received the ball, and putting in a short, swift shot, scored another goal for the Front, amid a tempest of hurrahings from the team and their supporters.

The game now stood three to one in favor of the Front, and up to the end of the first hour no change was made in this score.

And now there was a scene of the wildest enthusiasm and confusion. The Front people flocked upon the ice and carried off their team to their quarter of the shanty, loading them with congratulations and refreshing them with various drinks.

"Better get your men together, captain," suggested Craven, and Hughie gathered them into the Twentieth corner of the shanty.

In spite of the adverse score Hughie found his team full of fight. They crowded about him and the master, eager to listen to any explanation of the present defeat that might be offered for their comfort, or to any plans by which the defeat might be turned into victory. Some minutes they spent in excitedly discussing the various games, and in good-naturedly chaffing Thomas Finch for his failure to prevent a score. But Thomas had nothing to say in reply. He had done his best, and he had a feeling that they all knew it. No man was held in higher esteem by the team than the goal-keeper.

"Any plan, captain?" asked the master, after they had talked for some minutes, and all grew quiet.

"What do you think, sir?" said Hughie.

"O, let us hear from you. You're the captain."

"Well," said Hughie, slowly, and with deliberate emphasis, "I think we are going to win." (Yells from all sides.) "At any rate we ought to win, for I think we have the better team." (More yells.) "What I mean is this, I think we are better in combination play, and I don't think they have a man who can touch the master."

Enthusiastic exclamations, "That's right!" "Better believe it!" "Horo!"

"But we have a big fight before us. And that Dan Munro's a terror. The only change I can think of is to open out more and fall back from their goal for a little while. And then, if I can hold Dan--"

"Cries of "You'll hold him all right!" "You are the lad!"

"Everybody should feed the master. They can't stop him, any of them. But I would say for the first while, anyway, play defense. What do you think, sir?" appealing to the master.

"I call that good tactics. But don't depend too much upon me; if any man has a chance for a run and a shot, let him take it. And don't give up your combination in your forward line. The captain is quite right in seeking to draw them away from their goal. Their defense territory is too full now. Now, what I have noticed is this, they mainly rely upon Dan Munro and upon their three big defense men. For the first fifteen minutes they will make their hardest push. Let us take the captain's advice, fall back a little, and so empty their defense. But on the whole, keep your positions, play to your men, and," he added, with a smile, "don't get too mad."

"I guess they will be making some plans, too," said Thomas Finch, slowly, and everybody laughed.

"That's quite right, Thomas, but we'll give them a chance for the first while to show us what they mean to do."

At this point the minister came in, looking rather gloomy.

"Well, Mr. Craven, rather doubtful outlook, is it not?"

"O, not too bad, sir," said the master, cheerfully.

"Three to one. What worse do you want?"

"Well, six to one would be worse," replied the master. "Besides, their first two games were taken by a kind of fluke. We didn't know their play. You will notice they have taken only one in the last three-quarters of an hour."

"I doubt they are too big for you," continued the minister.

"Isn't altogether size that wins in shinny," said Mr. Craven. "Hughie there isn't a very big man, but he can hold any one of them."

"Well, I hope you may be right," said the minister. "I am sorry I have to leave the game to see a sick man up Kenyon way."

"Sorry you can't stay, sir, to see us win," said Craven, cheerfully, while Hughie slipped out to see his mother before she went.

"Well, my boy," said his mother, "you are playing a splendid game, and you are getting better as you go on."

"Thanks, mother. That's the kind of talk we like," said Hughie, who had been a little depressed by his father's rather gloomy views. "I'm awfully sorry you can't stay."

"And so am I, but we must go. But we shall be back in time for supper, and you will ask all the team to come down to celebrate their victory."

"Good for you, mother! I'll tell them, and I bet they'll play."

Meantime the team from the Front had been having something of a jollification in their quarters. They were sure of victory, and in spite of their captain's remonstrances had already begun to pass round the bottle in the way of celebration.

"They're having something strong in there," said little Mac McGregor. "Wish they'd pass some this way."

"Let them have it," said Johnnie Big Duncan, whose whole family ever since the revival had taken a total abstinence pledge, although this was looked upon as a very extreme position indeed, by almost all the community. But Big Duncan Campbell had learned by very bitter experience that for him, at least, there was no safety in a moderate use of "God's good creature," as many of his fellow church-members designated the "mountain dew," and his sons had loyally backed him up in this attitude.

"Quite, right!" said the master, emphatically. "And if they had any sense they would know that with every drink they are throwing away a big chance of winning."

"Horo, you fellows!" shouted big Hec Ross across to them, "aren't you going to play any more? Have you got enough of it already?"

"We will not be caring for any more of yon kind," said Johnnie Big Duncan, good-naturedly, "and we were thinking of giving you a change."

"Come away and be at it, then," said Hec, "for we're all getting cold."

"That's easily cured," said Dan, as they sallied forth to the ice again, "for I warrant you will not be suffering from the cold in five minutes."

When the teams took up their positions, it was discovered that Dan had fallen back to the center, and Hughie was at a loss to know how to meet this new disposition of the enemy's force.

"Let them go on," said the master, with whom Hughie was holding a hurried consultation. "You stick to him, and we'll play defense till they develop their plan."

The tactics of the Front became immediately apparent upon the drop of the ball, and proved to be what the master had foretold. No sooner had the game begun than the big defense men advanced with the centers to the attack, and when Hughie followed up his plan of sticking closely to Dan Munro and hampering him, he found Jimmie Ben upon him, swiping furiously with his club at his shins, with evident intention of intimidating him, as well as of relieving Dan from his attentions. But if Jimmie Ben thought by his noisy shouting and furious swiping to strike terror to the heart of the Twentieth captain, he entirely misjudged his man; for without seeking to give him back what he received in kind, Hughie played his game with such skill and pluck, that although he was considerably battered about the shins, he was nevertheless able to prevent Dan from making any of his dangerous rushes.

Craven, meantime, if he noticed Hughie's hard case, was so fully occupied with the defense of the goal that he could give no thought to anything else. Shot after shot came in upon Thomas at close range, and so savage and reckless was the charge of the Front that their big defense men, Hec Ross and Jimmie Ben, abandoning their own positions, were foremost in the melee before the Twentieth goal.

For fully fifteen minutes the ball was kept in the Twentieth territory, and only the steady coolness of Craven and Johnnie Big Duncan, backed by Hughie's persistent checking of the Front captain and the magnificent steadiness of Thomas in goal, saved the game.

At length, as the fury of the charge began to expend itself a little, Craven got his chance. The ball had been passed out to Dan upon the left wing of the Front forward line. At once Hughie was upon him, but Jimmie Ben following hard, with a cruel swipe at Hughie's skates, laid him flat, but not until he had succeeded in hindering to some degree Dan's escape with the ball. Before the Front captain could make use of his advantage and get clear away, the master bore down upon him like a whirlwind, hurled him clear off his feet, secured the ball, dashed up the open field, and eluding the two centers, who had been instructed to cover the goal, easily shot between the balsam-trees.

For a few moments the Twentieth men went mad, for they all felt that a crisis had been passed. The failure of the Front in what had evidently been a preconcerted and very general attack was accepted as an omen of victory.

The Front men, on the other hand, were bitterly chagrined. They had come so near it, and yet had failed. Jimmie Ben was especially savage. He came down the ice toward the center, yelling defiance and threats of vengeance. "Come on here! Don't waste time. Let us at them. We'll knock them clear off the ice."

It was Dan's drop. As he was preparing to face off, the master skated up and asked the umpire for time. At once the crowd gathered round.

"What's the matter?" "What's up?" "What do you want?" came on all sides from the Front team, now thoroughly aroused and thirsting for vengeance.

"Mr. Umpire," said the master, "I want to call your attention to a bit of foul play that must not be allowed to go on"; and then he described Jimmie Ben's furious attack upon Hughie.

"It was a deliberate trip, as well as a savage swipe at a man's shins when the ball was not near."

At once Jimmie Ben gave him the lie, and throwing down his club, slammed his cap upon the ice and proceeded to execute a war-dance about it.

For a few moments there was a great uproar, and then the master's voice was heard again addressing the umpire.

"I want to know your ruling upon this, Mr. Umpire"; and somehow his voice commanded a perfect stillness.

"Well," said the umpire, hesitating, "of course--if a man trips it is foul play, but--I did not see any tripping. And of course-- swiping at a man's shins is not allowed, although sometimes--it can't very well be helped in a scrimmage."

"I merely want to call your attention to it," said the master. "My understanding of our arrangements, Mr. Munro," he said, addressing the Front captain, "is that we are here to play shinny. You have come up here, I believe, to win the game by playing shinny, and we are here to prevent you. If you have any other purpose, or if any of your men have any other purpose, we would be glad to know it now, for we entered this game with the intention of playing straight, clean shinny."

"That's right!" called out Hec Ross; "that's what we're here for." And his answer was echoed on every side, except by Jimmie Ben, who continued to bluster and offer fight.

"O, shut your gab!" finally said Farquhar Bheg, impatiently. "If you want to fight, wait till after the game is done."

"Here's your cap, Jimmie," piped a thin, little voice. "You'll take cold in your head." It was little French Fusie, holding up Jimmie's cap on the end of his shinny club, and smiling with the utmost good nature, but with infinite impudence, into Jimmie's face.

At once there was a general laugh at Jimmie Ben's expense, who with a growl, seized his cap, and putting it on his head, skated off to his place.

"Now," said Hughie, calling his men together for a moment, "let us crowd them hard, and let's give the master every chance we can."

"No," said the master, "they are waiting for me. Suppose you leave Dan to me for a while. You go up and play your forward combination. They are not paying so much attention to you. Make the attack from your wing."

At the drop Dan secured the ball, and followed by Fusie, flew up the center with one of the Reds on either hand. Immediately the master crossed to meet him, checked him hard, and gave Fusie a chance, who, seizing the ball, passed far up to Hughie on the right.

Immediately the Twentieth forward line rushed, and by a beautiful hit of combined play, brought the ball directly before the Front goal, when Don, holding it for a moment till Hughie charged in upon Farquhar Bheg, shot, and scored.

The result of their combination at once inspired the Twentieth team with fresh confidence, and proved most disconcerting to their opponents.

"That's the game, boys," said the master, delightedly. "Keep your heads, and play your positions." And so well did the forward line respond that for the next ten minutes the game was reduced to a series of attacks upon the Front goal, and had it not been for the dashing play of their captain and the heavy checking of the Front defense, the result would have been most disastrous to them.

Meantime, the Twentieth supporters, lined along either edge, became more and more vociferous as they began to see that their men were getting the game well into their own hands. That steady, cool, systematic play of man to man was something quite new to those accustomed to the old style of game, and aroused the greatest enthusiasm.

Gradually the Front were forced to fall back into their territory, and to play upon the defensive, while the master and Johnnie Big Duncan, moving up toward the center, kept their forward line so strongly supported, and checked so effectually any attempts to break through, that thick and fast the shots fell upon the enemy's goal.

There remained only fifteen minutes to play. The hard pace was beginning to tell upon the big men, and the inevitable reaction following their unwise "celebrating" began to show itself in their stale and spiritless play. On the other hand, the Twentieth were as fresh as ever, and pressed the game with greater spirit every moment.

"Play out toward the side," urged Dan, despairing of victory, but determined to avert defeat, and at every opportunity the ball was knocked out of play. But like wolves the Twentieth forwards were upon the ball, striving to keep it in play, and steadily forcing it toward the enemy's goal.

Dan became desperate. He was wet with perspiration, and his breath was coming in hard gasps. He looked at his team. The little Reds were fit enough, but the others were jaded and pumped out. Behind him stood Jimmie Ben, savage, wet, and weary.

At one of the pauses, when the ball was out of play, Dan dropped on his knee.

"Hold on there a minute," he cried; "I want to fix this skate of mine."

Very deliberately he removed his strap, readjusted his skate, and began slowly to set the strap in place again.

"They want a rest, I guess. Better take off the time, umpire," sang out Fusie, dancing as lively as a cricket round Jimmie Ben, who looked as if he would like to devour him bodily.

"Shut up, Fusie!" said Hughie. "We've got all the time we need."

"You have, eh?" said Jimmie Ben, savagely.

"Yes," said Hughie, in sudden anger, for he had not forgotten Jimmie Ben's cruel swipe. "We don't need any more time than we've got, and we don't need to play any dirty tricks, either. We're going to beat you. We've got you beaten now."

"Blank your impudent face! Wait you! I'll show you!" said Jimmie Ben.

"You can't scare me, Jimmie Ben," said Hughie, white with rage. "You tried your best and you couldn't do it."

"Play the game, Hughie," said the master, in a low tone, skating round him, while Hec Ross said, good-naturedly, "Shut up Jimmie Ben. You'll need all your wind for your heels," at which all but Jimmie Ben laughed.

For a moment Dan drew his men together.

"Our only chance," he said, "is in a rush. Now, I want every man to make for that goal. Never mind the ball. I'll get the ball there. And then you, Jimmie Ben, and a couple of you centers, make right back here on guard."

"They're going to rush," said Hughie to his team. "Don't all go back. Centers fall back with me. You forwards keep up."

At the drop Dan secured the ball, and in a moment the Front rush came. With a simultaneous yell the whole ten men came roaring down the ice, waving their clubs and flinging aside their lightweight opponents. It was a dangerous moment, but with a cry of "All steady, boys!" Hughie threw himself right into Dan's way. But just for such a chance Jimmie Ben was watching, and rushing upon Hughie, caught him fairly with his shoulder and hurled him to the ice, while the attacking line swept over him.

For a single moment Hughie lay dazed, but before any one could offer help he rose slowly, and after a few deep breaths, set off for the scrimmage.

There was a wild five minutes. Eighteen or twenty men were massed in front of the Twentieth goal, striking, shoving, yelling, the solid weight of the Front defense forcing the ball ever nearer the goal. In the center of the mass were Craven, Johnnie Big Duncan, and Don fighting every inch.

For a few moments Hughie hovered behind his goal, his heart full of black rage, waiting his chance. At length he saw an opening. Jimmie Ben, slashing heavily, regardless of injury to himself or any others, had edged the ball toward the Twentieth left. Taking a short run, Hughie, reckless of consequences, launched himself head first into Jimmie Ben's stomach, swiping viciously at the same time at the ball. For a moment Jimmie Ben was flung back, and but for Johnnie Big Duncan would have fallen, but before he could regain his feet, the ball was set free of the scrimmage and away. Fusie, rushing in, had snapped it up and had gone scuttling down the ice, followed by Hughie and the master.

Before Fusie had got much past center, Dan, who had been playing in the rear of the scrimmage, overtook him, and with a fierce body check upset the little Frenchman and secured the ball. Wheeling, he saw both Hughie and Craven bearing down swiftly upon him.

"Rush for the goal!" he shouted to Jimmie Ben, who was following Hughie hard. Jimmie Ben hesitated.

"Back to your defense!" yelled Dan, cutting across and trying to escape between Hughie and Craven.

It was in vain. Both of the Twentieth men fell upon him, and the master, snatching the ball, sped like lightning down the ice.

The crowd went wild.

"Get back! Get back there!" screamed Hughie to the mob crowding in upon the ice. "Give us room! Give us a show!"

At this moment Craven, cornered by Hec Ross and two of the Red Shirts, with Dan hard upon his heels, passed clear across the ice to Hughie. With a swift turn Hughie caught the ball, dodged Jimmie Ben's fierce spring at him, and shot. But even as he shot, Jimmie Ben, recovering his balance, reached him and struck a hard, swinging blow upon his ankle. There was a sharp crack, and Hughie fell to the ice. The ball went wide.

"Time, there, umpire!" cried the master, falling on his knees beside Hughie. "Are you hurt, Hughie?" he asked, eagerly. "What is it, my boy?"

"Oh, master, it's broken, but don't stop. Don't let them stop. We must win this game. We've only a few minutes. Take me back to goal and send Thomas out."

The eager, hurried whisper, the intense appeal in the white face and dark eyes, made the master hesitate in his emphatic refusal.

"You can't--"

"Oh, don't stop! Don't stop it for me," cried Hughie, gripping the master's arm.

"Help me up and take me back."

The master swore a fierce oath.

"We'll do it, my boy. You're a trump. Here, Don," he called aloud, "we'll let Hughie keep goal for a little," and they ran Hughie back to the goal on one skate.

"You go out, Thomas," gasped Hughie. "Don't talk. We've only five minutes."

"They have broken his leg," said the master, with a sob in his voice.

"Nothing wrong, I hope," said Dan, skating up.

"No; play the game," said the master, fiercely. His black eyes were burning with a deep, red glow.

"Is it hurting much?" asked Thomas, lingering about Hughie.

"Oh, you just bet! But don't wait. Go on! Go on down! You've got to get this game!"

Thomas glanced at the foot hanging limp, and then at the white but resolute face. Then saying with slow, savage emphasis, "The brute beast! As sure as death I'll do for him," he skated off to join the forward line.

It was the Front knock-off from goal. There was no plan of attack, but the Twentieth team, looking upon the faces of the master and Thomas, needed no words of command.

The final round was shot, short, sharp, fierce. A long drive from Farquhar Bheg sent the ball far up into the Twentieth territory. It was a bad play, for it gave Craven and Thomas their chance.

"Follow me close, Thomas," cried the master, meeting the ball and setting off like a whirlwind.

Past the little Reds, through the centers, and into the defense line he flashed, followed hard by Thomas. In vain Hec Ross tried to check, Craven was past him like the wind. There remained only Dan and Jimmie Ben. A few swift strides, and the master was almost within reach of Dan's club. With a touch of the ball to Thomas he charged into his waiting foe, flung him aside as he might a child, and swept on.

"Take the man, Thomas," he cried, and Thomas, gathering himself up in two short, quick strikes, dashed hard upon Jimmie Ben, and hurled him crashing to the ice.

"Take that, you brute, you!" he said, and followed after Craven.

Only Farquhar Bheg was left.

"Take no chances," cried Craven again. "Come on!" and both of them sweeping in upon the goal-keeper, lifted him clear through the goal and carried the ball with them.

"Time!" called the umpire. The great game was won.

Then, before the crowd had realized what had happened, and before they could pour in upon the ice, Craven skated back toward Jimmie Ben.

"The game is over," he said, in a low, fierce tone. "You cowardly blackguard, you weren't afraid to hit a boy, now stand up to a man, if you dare."

Jimmie Ben was no coward. Dropping his club he came eagerly forward, but no sooner had he got well ready than Craven struck him fair in the face, and before he could fall, caught him with a straight, swift blow on the chin, and lifting him clear off his skates, landed him back on his head and shoulders on the ice, where he lay with his toes quivering.

"Serve him right," said Hec Ross.

There was no more of it. The Twentieth crowds went wild with joy and rage, for their great game was won, and the news of what had befallen their captain had got round.

"He took his city, though, Mrs. Murray," said the master, after the great supper in the manse that evening, as Hughie lay upon the sofa, pale, suffering, but happy. "And not only one, but a whole continent of them, and," he added, "the game as well."

With sudden tears and a little break in her voice, the mother said, looking at her boy, "It was worth while taking the city, but I fear the game cost too much."

"Oh, pshaw, mother," said Hughie, "it's only one bone, and I tell you that final round was worth a leg."

CHAPTER XV

THE RESULT

"How many did you say, Craven, of those Glengarry men of yours?" Professor Gray was catechizing his nephew.

"Ten of them, sir, besides the minister's son, who is going to take the full university course."

"And all of them bound for the ministry?"

"So they say. And judging by the way they take life, and the way, for instance, they play shinny, I have a notion they will see it through."

"They come of a race that sees things through," answered the professor. "And this is the result of this Zion Hill Academy I have been hearing so much about?"

"Well, sir, they put in a good year's work, I must say."

"You might have done worse, sir. Indeed, you deserve great credit, sir."

"I? Not a bit. I simply showed them what to do and how to do it. But there's a woman up there that the world ought to know about. For love of her--"

"Oh, the world!" snorted the professor. "The world, sir! The Lord deliver us! It might do the world some good, I grant."

"It is for love of her these men are in for the ministry."

"You are wrong, sir. That is not their motive."

"No, perhaps it is not. It would be unfair to say so, but yet she--"

"I know, sir. I know, sir. Bless my soul, sir. I know her. I knew her before you were born. But--yes, yes--" the professor spoke as if to himself--"for love of her men would attempt great things. You have these names, Craven? Ah! Alexander Stewart, Donald Cameron, Thomas Finch--Finch, let me see--ah, yes, Finch. His mother died after a long illness. Yes, I remember. A very sad case, a very sad case, indeed."

"And yet not so sad, sir," put in Craven. "At any rate, it did not seem so at the time. That night it seemed anything but sad. It was wonderful."

The professor laid down his list and sat back in his chair.

"Go on, sir," he said, gazing curiously at Craven. "I have heard a little about it. Let me see, it was the night of the great match, was it not?"

"Did you know about that? Who told you about the match, sir?"

"I hear a great many things, and in curious ways. But go on, sir, go on."

Craven sat silent, and from the look in his eyes his thoughts were far away.

"Well, sir, it's a thing I have never spoken about. It seems to me, if I may say so, something quite too sacred to speak of lightly."

Again Craven paused, while the professor waited.

"It was Hughie sent me there. There was a jubilation supper at the manse, you understand. Thomas Finch, the goal-keeper, you know-- magnificent fellow, too--was not at the supper. A messenger had come for him, saying that his mother had taken a bad turn. Hughie was much disappointed, and they were all evidently anxious. I offered to drive over and inquire, and of course the minister's wife, though she had been on the go all day long, must needs go with me. I can never forget that night. I suppose you have noticed, sir, there are times when one is more sensitive to impressions from one's surroundings than others. There are times with me, too, when I seem to have a very vital kinship with nature. At any rate, during that drive nature seemed to get close to me. The dark, still forest, the crisp air, the frost sparkling in the starlight on the trees--it all seemed to be part of me. I fear I am not explaining myself."

Craven paused again, and his eyes began to glow. The professor still waited.

"When we reached the house we found them waiting for death. The minister's wife went in, I waited in the kitchen. By and by Billy Jack, that's her eldest son, you know, came out. 'She is asking for you,' he said, and I went in. I had often seen her before, and I rather think she liked me. You see, I had been able to help Thomas along pretty well, both in school and with his night work, and she was grateful for what I had done, absurdly grateful when one considers how little it was. I had seen death before, and it had always been ghastly, but there was nothing ghastly in death that night. The whole scene is before me now, I suppose always will be."

His dead, black eyes were beginning to show their deep, red fire.

The professor looked at him for a moment or two, and then said, "Proceed, if you please," and Craven drew a long breath, as if recalling himself, and went on.

"The old man was there at one side, with his gray head down on the bed, his little girl kneeling beside him with her arm round his neck, opposite him the minister's wife, her face calm and steady, Billy Jack standing at the foot of the bed--he and little Jessac the only ones in the room who were weeping--and there at the head, Thomas, supporting his mother, now and then moistening her lips and giving her sips of stimulant, and so quick and steady, gentle as a woman, and smiling through it all. I could hardly believe it was the same big fellow who three hours before had carried the ball through the Front defense. I tell you, sir, it was wonderful.

"There was no fuss or hysterical nonsense in that room. The mother lay there quite peaceful, pain all gone--and she had had enough of it in her day. She was quite a beautiful woman, too, in a way. Fine eyes, remarkable eyes, splendidly firm mouth, showing great nerve, I should say. All her life, I understand, she lived for others, and even now her thought was not of herself. When I came in she opened her eyes. They were like stars, actually shining, and her smile was like the sudden breaking of light through a cloud. She put out her hand for mine, and said--and I value these words, sir--'Mr. Craven, I give you a mither's thanks and a mither's blessing for a' you have done for ma laddie.' She was Lowland Scotch, you know. My voice went all to pieces. I tried to say it was nothing, but stuck. Thomas helped me out, and without a shake or quiver in his voice, he answered for me.

"'Yes, indeed, mother, we'll not forget it.'

"'And perhaps you can help him a bit still. He will be needing it,' she added.

"I assure you, sir, that quiet steadiness of Thomas and herself braced me up, and I was able to make my promise. And then she said, with a look that somehow reminded me of the deep, starlit night outside, through which I had just come, 'And you, Mr. Craven, you will give your life to God?'

"Again my voice failed me. It was so unexpected, and quite overwhelming. Once more Thomas answered for me.

"'Yes, mother, he will, sure,' and she seemed to take it as my promise, for she smiled again at me, and closed her eyes.

"I had read of triumphant death-bed scenes, and all that before, without taking much stock in them, but believe me, sir, that room was full of glory. The very faces of those people, it seemed to me, were alight. It may be imagination, but even now, as I think of it, it seems real. There were no farewells, no wailing, and at the very last, not even tears. Thomas, who had nursed her for more than a year, still supported her, the smile on his face to the end. And the end--"Craven's voice grew unsteady--"it is difficult to speak of. The minister's wife repeated the words about the house with many mansions, and those about the valley of the shadow, and said a little prayer, and then we all waited for the end--for myself, I confess with considerable fear and anxiety. I had no need to fear. After a long silence she sat up straight, and in her Scotch tongue, she said, with a kind of amazed joy in her tone, 'Ma fayther! Ma fayther! I am here.' Then she settled herself back in her son's arms, drew a deep breath, and was still. All through the night and next day the glory lingered round me. I went about as in a strange world. I am afraid you will be thinking me foolish, sir."

The stern old professor was openly wiping his eyes. He seemed quite unable to find his voice. At length he took up the list again, and began to read it mechanically.

"What! What's this?" he said, suddenly, pointing to a name on the list.

"That, sir, is John Craven."

"Do you mean that you, too--"

"Yes, I mean it, if you think I am fit."

"Fit, Jack, my boy! None of us are fit. But what--how did this come?" The professor blew his nose like a trumpet.

"That I can hardly tell myself," said Craven, with a kind of wonder in his voice; "but at any rate it is the result of my Glengarry School Days."

THE END